Great Balls of Fire

A Year of Scottish Festivals

Gary Sutherland

BIRLINN

This edition first published in 2009 by
Birlinn Limited
West Newington House
10 Newington Road
Edinburgh
EH9 1QS

www.birlinn.co.uk

ISBN: 978 1 84158 768 4

British Library Cataloguing-in-Publication Data
A catalogue record for this book is available from the British Library

Typeset by Iolaire Typesetting, Newtonmore
Printed and bound by CPI Cox & Wyman, Reading

For my girls,

Clare and Isabella Rose

CONTENTS

About a Ba'

New Year began not with a bang but a whimper, a tear in my eye and a lump in my throat. Slumped on a couch in Kirkwall, I wasn't having the best of Hogmanays. Mostly I was thinking about my dad. He'd passed away barely a month ago. Helping me through a dark night in Orkney were my wife, Clare, and my friend Brian. Their warm company would stop me from wallowing too much in self-pity. Watching the rubbish on the telly wasn't doing any of us much good. New Year TV had always depressed me.

It was a pity. I'd really been looking forward to spending New Year up here. My mind had been full of plans and places in Scotland I'd never seen before. I was upbeat about my year of living ceremoniously, visiting various festivals throughout the country. What are festivals if not celebrations? My next twelve months would be defined by them. Then my dad died and my party hat went in the bin.

Somehow, my mam, my brother Stewart, my sister Julieann and I got through Christmas together. I roasted the turkey, though I have no memory of doing so. We ate, drank and remembered James Alexander Sutherland. We coped better than I thought we would. I think we were just numb enough to manage. Now it was harder. And my folks were hundreds of miles away, back in Hopeman. How were they coping with the unwelcome Bells and the unrelenting pain? I'd phone home in a bit. 'Happy New Year.' I'd say it anyway. New Year is so often an anti-climax, but this was so much worse.

Lost in thought in a strange hired cottage. In approximately twelve hours' time, my year of witnessing traditional Scottish events would get off to a boisterous start with The Ba'. Dad would have loved The Ba', I'm sure of it. I'd been expecting him to accompany me on some of my travels. Dad thrived on the occasion and was more often than not the life of the party. Now he was gone. How do you cope with that loss? What was I even doing here? Working on a book was the obvious answer. But what was I *doing* here? I should have been with my mam. What did all this matter? At least Clare and Brian were here. I'd never have managed on my own.

I fancied some fresh air. Best get up off this couch and move away from the box. I could hear fireworks outside. It would be a shame to miss them. It was time to give up the warmth of the living room and try to clear my head. I turned to Clare. 'Let's watch the fireworks.' She smiled. 'That would be good.' Brian was on his feet already. The three of us walked out into the cold night. The fireworks danced over Kirkwall Bay. They were pretty. It almost felt like New Year. For a moment, I forgot. 'They're amazing,' I said. 'Happy New Year,' said Brian, handing me a dram from his hipflask. 'Cheers Brian, Happy New Year.' I put the whisky to my lips and warmed my heart. 'I'd like to join you,' sighed Clare. But she'd have to sit this one out. My wife was five months pregnant with our first child. I would be a dad soon. Life was changing fast; not everything was bad. 'Happy New Year,' I said, kissing Clare. What a year lay ahead of us – never mind all these festivals.

'Let's go back inside,' I suggested. 'Big day tomorrow.'

'You mean today,' Clare corrected me.

'Aye, today. It'll be good, won't it?'

'You'll enjoy it.'

'It sounds mad,' said Brian.

*　　*　　*

I was in serious danger of being dashed against the wall by a human tornado. I had to get out of harm's way. The excitement of being close to the eye of the storm was one thing, but I hadn't come all the way to Orkney to be trampled on. Topping off my New Year trip with footprints on my head was not my idea of fun and neither was spending the night in hospital. I didn't want to be some latter-day Humpty Dumpty they couldn't put back together again. Better to keep my wits about me and my body in working order, maintain a safe distance and watch in awe. Why should I be done for when the pack broke? Rattled by the rush and faced with the threat of all hell breaking loose, I beat a hasty retreat, like the scaredy custard I am.

The Uppies and Doonies were barely ten minutes into their New Year bash on the cobblestones of Kirkwall. A few hundred Orcadian men were literally letting off steam, their contorted faces turning redder by the minute. This almighty street battle wasn't for the weak-willed. You had to be strong-minded and hard as nails. You had to be mad as a shipment of frogs. I hung back and shook my head in admiration as one half of town laid into the other. The Uppies and Doonies would fight until the bitter end. Nothing else mattered. It was all about The Ba'.

If you're an Uppie or a Doonie, you dream of winning the ba' and keeping it forever. To carry it home is a thrill without compare. Each time The Ba' is played, some bold and deserving individual makes a successful bid for it and a lifelong ambition is realized. On Christmas Day, and again on New Year's Day, The Ba' dominates the minds of the men of Kirkwall. On Christmas Day, Christmas dinner is secondary. The Ba' is the main event. On New Year's Day, you don't lie in bed with a hangover sweating out the excesses of the night before. You get up and you march to the Mercat Cross to play The Ba'. Hogmanay in Kirkwall is a low-key affair, because it's overshadowed by The Ba', the local obsession they just can't shake off.

As rivalries go, it doesn't get fiercer than the Uppies and the Doonies. The Uppies hate being beaten by the Doonies and the Doonies can't stand the Uppies having the upper-hand. It's like Rangers and Celtic, but older, more palatable and more up-close-and-personal. The Uppies must work the ba' to the top of the town and make it touch the gable end at Mackison's Corner. The Doonies need to land the ba' in Kirkwall Bay. The Ba' is a game that can last several hours. These northern warriors are in it for the long-haul. And, today, so was I, as an untrained observer. Clare and Brian had watched the start, the throw-up, but had opted not to spend the rest of the afternoon watching grown men fight in the streets. Instead, they'd gone off in the hire car to check out some standing stones. I'd have to save them for another time. They weren't going anywhere.

The Ba' begins in the shadow of the magnificent St Magnus Cathedral at the Mercat Cross. It used to be that if you were born north of the cross, you were an Uppie and, if you entered the world south of it, you were deemed to be a Doonie. It's not such a hard-and-fast rule nowadays. The location of the local hospital would only produce a steady stream of Uppies, if the old demarcation line held true. No, in more modern times, it's more to do with family loyalty. You play for the same side as your forefathers. And no matter where you happen to live, whether you work elsewhere in Orkney, or further afield, if the connection is strong, you return year after year, with your loyalty and your pride, and you give your all for The Ba'.

In the football matches of my childhood, down on the Hopeman pitch after school, you'd often hear the cry 'My ba'!' or shout it yourself as you shot for glory. How good those games were. A few of us would meet outside Miele's café, decide we fancied a game and, by the time we'd reached the bottom of Harbour Street, word had spread. Boys would come running from all corners of the village and soon there would be enough for five-a-side, sometimes not far off eleven. Captains were nominated and would pick teams from the line of hopefuls. We played with boundless energy – and no little skill, in some cases – until it got dark. Then my brother and I would go home to face the wrath of Mam. She didn't mind us playing football till all hours but she did mind us coming home with our jeans clarted in mud. We didn't see the big deal but now we realise the amount of extra washing we created for her. Back then though, it seemed more important that we'd had a good game and maybe scored a few goals.

Fitba's one thing; The Ba' is something else entirely. I didn't grow up Kirkwall. If I had, I might have been part of this. I can't quite imagine being brave enough. I could kick a ba', but play for The Ba'? It's the mother of all contests, like an extreme version of rugby, but with hundreds in a scrum that never seems to end. At first sight, The Ba' is an unruly spectacle. There don't appear to be any rules. It looks downright dangerous and *is* downright dangerous. Chaos and disorder reign in what is, without doubt, a man's game. It's rowdy beyond belief. The combatants get all hot and bothered about a ba' most of them can't even see. It's buried in there somewhere among the writhing bodies. And the pitch isn't a patch of grass. The pitch is Kirkwall. The path to victory is through its narrow streets and lanes and, occasionally, the rooftops. There's no out-of-bounds with The Ba'. They're out of their minds. Never mind the namby-pamby Old Firm; live and unleashed, from Kirkwall, comes The Ba'. That such a tiny word – Ba' – could carry such huge meaning.

On the eve of The Ba', in the hours leading up to the Bells, I dropped by the home of the Gibson family, deep in Uppie territory, not far from the gable end at Mackison's Corner. The Gibsons are not only Ba' players, they're the ba' makers. To say that Gary and his sons Edgar and Sigurd are steeped in The Ba' is an understatement. From them, I learned how the ba' is made and how The Ba' is won. The Gibsons have form: Gary, Edgar and Sigurd have enjoyed tremendous success in The Ba' over the years.

Edgar is a gentle giant (when he's not grappling for the ba'). With those broad shoulders, he's built for The Ba'. You wouldn't want to be facing Edgar. You'd want him on your side. Edgar and Gary – whose Ba'-playing days are behind him; he's in his seventies now – showed me the ba' and explained the painstaking but loving process of making one by hand. The game may seem ugly, but the ba' itself is beautiful. It's an exquisite piece of craftsmanship. As an object, the ba' can't help but draw the eye, with its rich black and brown leather panels. It's bigger – and a few pounds heavier – than a football. If anything, it resembles a medicine ball. It's tough, too. It has to be for the routine beating it takes. The ba' must be rock-hard to withstand the intense pressure of the pack. The ba' is packed with cork dust. If the Doonies win and the ba' ends up in the sea, it'll float. Each Ba' game requires a new ba', since the winner takes it home. The beauty of the ba' isn't easy to achieve – the stitching alone takes a couple of days – but it's clearly a labour of love for Edgar who, like his younger brother Sigurd, learned the art of ba' making from a master: their dad.

Edgar had made the ba' for tomorrow's game and was delighted with it. The perfectionist is content when he attains perfection. Edgar's latest effort had been displayed in the window of Sutherland the Chemist for all to admire in the run up to the New Year Ba'. He estimated it takes him around 140 hours in total to finish a ba'. 'You might do it five days on the trot or for a couple of hours at night,' said Edgar, who makes the ba' in Glasgow, where he lives and works. When he lived in London, he made the ba' there. Edgar produced his first ba' as a teenager, when his dad was one of the main ba' makers. Gary started in the mid-60s and, by the time he stopped three decades later, had made 45 of them. 'No two ba's are identical,' said Gary. 'If you threw a dozen ba's on the floor, the ba' winners would be able to pick oot their own.' I turned to Edgar sitting beside me and asked him if the ba's are indestructible. 'I hope so!' he laughed. Only one had ever burst, to Gary's knowledge, and that was before his time.

Edgar was bursting with pride when he won his men's ba'. (He'd already bagged his boys' ba', the Boys' Ba' game taking place on the mornings of Christmas Day and New Year's Day, before the men leap into action.) 'It's like the ultimate,' said Edgar. 'It's just a massive thing.' Everything had been building up to that sweet moment and when it arrived Edgar was on top of the world, as well as the shoulders of his fellow Uppies. Edgar had debuted in the Men's Ba' when he was fourteen. 'You can play the Boys' Ba' till you're fifteen, but I won it at fourteen, which was quite unusual. So I started the Men's Ba' the week after. My last year in the Boys' Ba', I played all four games. Boys' Ba' morning, Men's Ba' afternoon.' I don't imagine Edgar had much difficulty with that busy workload. Fittingly, the boys' ba' he won had been made by his dad.

Winners of the Men's Ba' tend to be men in their mid-to-late thirties, according to Edgar, who fell into that bracket. 'You'd have to play for quite a while before you'd be considered.' Once the ba' touches the gable end or lands in the water, candidates from the winning team make their claims for the ba'. It's like a mini-election. The ba' is awarded to a player who is considered, by his team-mates, to have played a key role over a period of years and whose time has finally come. 'The team has a discussion of sorts,' explained Edgar. 'You can put yourself forward, but other players might say "No, I think he should get it." So you get players supporting different people. You tend to find that players start to put their name in and have a bit of a shout for it maybe a couple of years before they really think they'll get it. It's putting your hat into the ring. You'll maybe start with four contenders and after five minutes a couple of them will drop oot. Then it will sort of come down to the main two contenders.'

'A lot of very good players never get a ba',' said Gary, 'because there are only two a year and you've got a whole lot of men the same age playing at the same time. So you need to have full attendance. You need to have been there for years and also you need to be an effective player before you'd be considered. There are fellas who would play a' their life and never be considered.'

While I was listening to them I suddenly felt envious of Edgar. It was simple enough. There he was sitting with his dad. And I didn't have that pleasure any more. For a moment, I let the sadness wash over me. Then my melancoholy passed and I was okay again. There was no point having thoughts that were no help to me, even if I couldn't help it. It was better to be thinking about The Ba'. I returned to the world where everything was fine.

Gary won the Men's Ba' back in 1967. His dad – Edgar's grandfather – won a ba' too. There were years when Gary and Edgar played together. It's the way. The family that plays together wins together (and sometimes loses together). Edgar played alongside Gary until his dad decided to call it a day. 'In the end, you get too old for it,' smiled Gary, who only really gave up The Ba' a few years ago. Edgar recalled his dad's final appearance. 'He wasna going to be playing, but he saw something happening and joined in. Next thing you know you end up face-to-face with him again!' Gary would still be jumping into the pack now if he could. 'I had a heart operation last summer so that's buggered me up. I can't go in the game noo. I dinna watch it either. I jist go doon for the throw-up and I come home.'

I was curious about the beating the body must take during The Ba'. Edgar was still sore from Christmas Day. 'I'm black and blue and all strapped up.' At least he hadn't got himself in the state he was in three years ago. 'I fractured me skull,' said Edgar matter-of-factly. 'The Doonies made a break for it and there wis aboot four or five of them running with the ba' and I sort of stopped them. I tackled them, basically. But I went ower and me head hit the corner o the kerb. I was in the hospital. I missed the New Year's game.'

Edgar totted up the breaks he'd suffered down the years. 'Fingers . . . ribs . . . when you're in the pack, the pressure's tremendous. If you get stuck in a lane or if you get caught against a barricade or a windowsill or a drainpipe or anything . . . you get a lot of that. Christmas Day there, there were six people taken away by the ambulance. There was one guy who was jist really crushed and couldna get breathin'. We had to stop for him. They jist came in and stood on top of everybody. There was a guy standing on the side of me head liftin' the other guy oot.'

I wondered if there was any danger attached to watching The Ba'. There was. Edgar told the tale of a sorry spectator a few years back. 'The guy was jist up here on holiday and he was watching it. He was wearing trainers and the ba' came flying oot o the pack and landed at his feet. He was supporting the Doonies and he jist thought he would leather it back doon the road, and he went like that.' Edgar mimicked a kick. 'And the ba' never went anywhere. He sort of broke two of his toes.' Edgar then issued a warning to me, a warning I'd do well to heed. 'The game can surge any time. There's a big crowd and you have to watch what you're doing.'

The Doonies had been feeling sore lately. They were enduring a barren time of it and the Uppies were heavily favoured for tomorrow's game. But Edgar was paying no heed to that. In his experience, it's cyclical. When the young Edgar was introduced to the Men's Ba', the Uppies were on a serious downer. He had to stomach being on the losing side 24 times out of his first 26 games, while the Doonies racked up a formidable run of results.

Now the steel-toe boot was on the other foot and the Uppies were dominant. Edgar had figured out his overall stats in The Ba' up to this point. 'I'm forty-five years old and I'm still four behind. I've lost more than I've won. I've lost thirty-three and won twenty-nine.' Even if the Uppies had been spoiled with success in recent years, Edgar was still making up lost ground. He could identify with the Doonies being in the doldrums at the moment, because it hadn't exactly been a barrel of laughs during his early days as an Uppie. 'The Doonies now are the way we were,' said Edgar. 'It gets very bitter. It's just because you've been getting beaten for so long. If you get beat on Christmas Day, you've only to wait a week for the chance to put it right. If you get beat on New Year's Day, you wait a whole year for revenge.'

'When you've been on the losing side a while,' said Gary, 'it's a hell of a long time.' Edgar continued: 'A team that's down can be a desperate team. Sometimes, when you're being beaten, one of the tactics you use is to try and get the game stuck somewhere until it gets dark, so that you've got a chance to smuggle the ba'.' Smuggling is the sneakiest of tactics employed in The Ba'. It's the trick up the sleeve, the ba' up the jumper. Sometimes it works, sometimes it doesn't. 'Aye,' laughed Gary. 'You try and slip away before anyone's noticed.' The Ba' demands honest effort, but deception plays a part in it.

Comparing The Ba' now to how it was in his heyday, Gary thought it as strong as ever – stronger if anything, especially at the start. 'When I was playing, the actual throw-up wasna so important. You'd have a lot of guys sort of strolling down an hour after the game started and joining in. Whereas now, they're all there at the throw-up. We never had anything like the number that's there now.'

There's tremendous support for The Ba' from the people of Kirkwall. The politicians haven't always embraced the rough-and-tumble nature of it. 'But fortunately,' said Edgar, 'we've got very good support from the present chief executive of Orkney Council. That's why he has been given the honour of throwing up the ba' tomorrow.'

Five ba's hang in the living-room window of the Gibson family home. 'Some people hang them up like this,' said Gary, 'or put them on their sideboard to show them off.' Later on, as I walked through the streets of Kirkwall, I'd notice one or two ba's in the front windows of other previous ba' winners. Gary and Edgar talked me through the five that had pride of place in their household. There was Gary's men's ba' from Christmas Day 1967, his boys' ba' from New Year's Day 1949, Edgar's men's ba' from Christmas Day 1999, his boys' ba' from Christmas Day 1976, and Sigurd's boys' ba' from Christmas Day 1985. One more and the set would be complete. Sigurd was on the case.

Sigurd was coming down the staircase now. He's shorter than his elder brother, but stocky. I'd have the pair of them on my side so I could hide behind them. Sigurd, like Edgar – and me for that matter – lives in Glasgow. We discovered that Sigurd and I don't live that far apart in the city. 'You'd have been cheaper jist coming roon the corner,' said Sigurd, 'but then you wouldn't't've got yer jolly up here!' I asked the Gibsons if they had any special Hogmanay plans, bearing in mind there was The Ba' tomorrow. Unsurprisingly, the men of Kirkwall don't overdo it after the Bells. 'People generally look after themselves at Hogmanay,' said Sigurd. 'The boys jist go to their beds. It's jist not worth it. You're going to be dehydrated anyway.'

Would the Uppies win again tomorrow? 'No idea,' said Edgar. 'You never know. In the big Doonie run they won twelve and, after the final one, we came away thinking "We'll never go up the street" – and we won the week afterwards. We were so well beaten on the Christmas Day we never thought we could win the next one, but we smuggled it.' The secret of success, emphasised Gary, was teamwork. 'If you get a team that's all disjointed and doesn't know what each other is going to do, then they lose.' Edgar agreed. 'It's a team thing. You get more senior players shouting or doing stuff, but it's down to the whole team.'

Having already been treated to an eye-watering account of Edgar's cracked skull, I asked Sigurd if he'd suffered any injuries. 'My pride,' he said. 'You get a few scrapes and cuts, but that's part and parcel of it.' Gary, speaking from many years of experience, said: 'You never notice if you win – and you feel pretty sore and battered if you lose.' Sigurd winced at the memory of the big Doonie run when the Uppies were forever up against it. 'The pain I felt when we were getting beat the whole time. Then, the first time we won, I was waiting for the pain and thinking "This is strange". It wisna there. We won, and there was no pain. When you're getting battered and going in the wrong direction, you're taking more knocks.' Sigurd had just provided a very good definition of a sore loser. He then explained to me why you can only ever win the Men's Ba' once in your lifetime. 'If you beat three hundred men and win the ba' you've then got to feed them wi drink all night. So you widna want to be doing it more than once.'

I thanked the Gibsons for their time and wished Edgar and Sigurd good luck in the New Year's Day Ba'. 'I bet you say that to everybody,' quipped Sigurd. He had a nice line in dry humour. I really liked the Gibsons. Before I'd met them, I'd been considering rooting for the Doonies. They were down on their luck, after all. But now I wanted Edgar and Sigurd to win. And I wanted Sigurd to get his men's ba'. I was siding with the Uppies. Really it was none of my business who won. I was simply an outsider. But it was too easy to take sides – and clearly very easy for me to swap sides. What a dreadful turncoat I was.

I waved goodbye to the Gibsons and walked back into town to pick up a few last-minute provisions before the shops shut for

New Year. A steak pie was obtained from the butcher and a few beers from the off-licence. I also popped into the tourist office and chatted to the nice man behind the desk about The Ba'. He confirmed that the real Ba' diehards are 'fairly abstemious' on Hogmanay but that they made up for it on the first. Back on the street, two teenage boys strutted past, getting tanked up on Buckfast. This disappointed me, seeing the tonic wine of the monks exerting an influence this far north. Buckfast is a common enough sight on the streets of Glasgow – but Kirkwall? Surely they should be on the Skullsplitter if they are planning on getting hammered in the daytime. Aside from the Buckfast mini-brigade, everything was winding down in Kirkwall. Everyone was heading home. It was the calm before the storm. I thought about tomorrow's Ba' and tried to imagine the outcome. It sounded like the Doonies might be in for more disappointment.

Now I had to go to the pub. I had it on good authority from journalist and Doonie Robert Leslie that his lot were having an eve-of-The-Ba' team meeting at Doonie HQ, the St Ola Hotel, by the harbour. I wouldn't be allowed anywhere near the meeting – in case I passed on valuable secrets to the Uppies – but it was a chance to meet Robert, who I'd only talked to on the phone. Robert said I'd recognise him by his generous beard. He was growing it especially for Up-Helly-Aa in Lerwick at the end of January. Robert was in Kirkwall City Pipe Band. They'd been invited up to Shetland to play at the annual Viking procession. The beard would help Robert blend in better with the hirsute Vikings. I was also going to Up-Helly-Aa but I'd left it far too late to cultivate a massive manly beard. Mine would look rubbish. I would stick to shaving.

I slipped into the St Ola and sat down in the corner with a pint. The bar was pretty much empty. After a while, a couple of men nipped in. Then, before I knew it, the place was heaving with Doonies. Sitting on my lonesome, looking out for a man with a big beard, I felt like I was under the glare of scrutiny. Certainly I was the subject of a couple of side-glances. The air reeked of secrecy and I was polluting it (in my paranoid mind at least). I was surely under suspicion of being an interloper, an Uppie spy, the worst possible thing. Then, to my relief, Robert turned up with his beard and we chatted for a bit. I had a friend and was no longer the enemy in their midst. Robert was hopeful the Doonies could do themselves justice tomorrow, though he knew it would be hard. Then it was time for the all-important meeting. Robert and all the other Doonies disappeared through the back of the bar to the lounge. I was alone with my pint again. After a while I had to go to the toilet. Naturally, the toilet was right next to the lounge. Through the frosted glass of the lounge door I could make out figures and could hear voices. If anyone left the lounge right now I'd be rumbled and charged with the heinous crime of eavesdropping on the Doonies as they discussed their tactics for The Ba', even though I was doing no such thing. After my trip to the men's room, I hurried back to the bar, sank my pint and left the pub to catch up with Clare and Brian. I was looking forward to that steak pie and maybe letting them have some of it. I'd worked up quite an appetite over the course of the afternoon.

On New Year's morning, Clare, Brian and I walked through the winding streets of Kirkwall towards the Mercat Cross for the throw-up of The Ba'. There was an eerie feeling about the place, which had a lot to do with the fact that everything was boarded up. Overnight they had battened down the hatches in Kirkwall. Windows and doors were barricaded with planks of wood, such were the protective measures taken by edgy shopkeepers and proud homeowners. These precautions were necessary. The Uppies and Doonies would be on the rampage soon. Kirkwall was bracing itself. It put me in mind of Pamplona before the running of the bulls. I wondered whether I'd rather take my chances with a few raging bulls or a few hundred stampeding Orcadians. In all honesty, I'd probably be better off with the bulls.

Even the cash machine was boarded up. I had to lean over the plank to punch in my card number. It was an awkward procedure, but I managed. I liked the fact that the tourist office was blockaded too. 'We'll have none of your stupid questions today, thanks.' It was a cold and dull day. A crowd was gathering on the Kirk Green in front of the cathedral. 'The Light of the North' – Kirkwall's central landmark – is 900 years old and looking good for its age. A German film crew was busying about, getting ready to capture footage of Das Ba'. All eyes were on Broad Street for the arrival of the Uppies and the Doonies. The Uppies turned up first, striding confidently in their assorted football and rugby shirts. There are no team colours in The Ba'. You wear what you like. You're expected to know whose side you're on and to know thine enemy. You can't be mistaking an Uppie for a Doonie. I noticed that a lot of the Uppies had their jeans strapped at the bottom with duct tape. The Uppies reached the Cross and waited for their age-old rivals. The Uppies looked like they meant business, the business of victory. Then came the Doonies, marching from the opposite direction. They looked just as defiant and confident. There were handshakes all round as Uppies and Doonies wished each other a Happy New Year. I hadn't expected this display of friendliness, but then how could it be otherwise? They would spend the rest of the day fighting each other. This seasonal spirit would soon wear off.

The Uppies had triumphed on Christmas Day with a breakaway. The winning move saw the ba' smuggled with the Uppies completing the job at Mackison's Corner almost four hours after the throw-up. Several of the players had ended up in hospital and at one point the ba' ended up on a roof. The facts showed that the Uppies were the form team. Aside from the New Year's game two years previously, when the Doonies had pinched it, the Uppies had claimed every Ba' since Christmas 1998. It was a long stretch, especially if you happened to be a Doonie.

The Boys' Ba' – the apprenticeship for the Men's Ba' but also very much an event in its own right – is often unresolved by the time the Men's Ba' begins. But today it was done and dusted shortly after midday when, following a two-hour tussle, the Uppies prevailed at the gable end with fifteen-year-old Kit Bichan claiming his boys' ba'.

Back at the Cross, the crowd and, more importantly, the Uppies and Doonies awaited the cathedral bell and the one o'clock throw-up of the ba'. The teams, one huddled mass, were poised, their necks craning, their arms outstretched for the first act in what promised to be an intense afternoon of rugged drama. The man handed the honour of throwing-up the ba' was Alistair Buchan, Orkney Islands Council's chief executive. The task is usually entrusted to a Ba' veteran but, from time to time, a public figure is invited to perform the duty, especially if they are a genuine supporter of The Ba', like Alistair. When approached by a group of senior Ba' players, Alistair had been only too happy to oblige. It was like a football fan being asked to kick off the World Cup Final.

'Come on, Alistair, throw it to the Doonies,' shouted a Doonie supporter. But Alistair's throw-up was fair and perfect, the ba' dropping into the middle of the pack as the players rose to meet it. The ba' was in the belly of the beast, where it would remain for most of the day.

Alistair admitted to being slightly overwhelmed by the occasion but was relieved to have done himself justice with his throw-up. 'This is the crowning glory of my career as far as I'm concerned. There is no bigger honour. It's a once-in-a-lifetime-experience. As an Orcadian, it is difficult to think of anything that is more powerful than that. I'm totally moved and overcome and I shall treasure this memory for the rest of my days.' He was keen to point out the uniqueness of The Ba' and argued it should never be taken for granted. 'I don't think you see it anywhere else. It's just special. It's about community and people being together and I think it's hard to beat. It's a spectacular setting with the cathedral behind us and in these days when people are so worried about overregulation and everything, here is a situation where the community is saying "This is what we're going to do" and that's it. And I think that's wonderful.' Alistair had one final word to describe the act of throwing up the ba' to the pack: 'Awesome.'

The madness had begun. The enormous pack swayed back and forth across Broad Street in a monumental display of single-bloody-mindedness. It takes two to tango but it requires three hundred to perform this demented Kirkwallian fling, this feeding frenzy to the thunderous soundtrack of heavy boots on the cobblestones. The Ba' men were ravenous for the ba'. To say there was pushing and shoving would be a huge understatement. The pack was one relentless entity daring anything to step in its path. Yet, after twenty minutes, the pack was pretty much where it had started. There was no quarter given and no ground being ceded cheaply. The lack of progress didn't dim the crowd's enthusiasm. 'Come on Uppies!' This was swiftly countered with the cry of 'Come on Doonies!' Some of the spectators wore hats with 'Uppie' or 'Doonie' on them, so that there would be no doubting their allegiance.

Veteran Ba' players on the cusp of the pack barked instructions to crushed team-mates. 'There's yer ba' right there!' 'Never turn yer back!' Some of the older heads coached from on top of the wall at the Kirk Green, benefiting from a better vantage point. There were a lot of cryptic hand signals being flashed. Brute force alone won't win you The Ba'. You need crafty tactics. There's a certain reliance on trickery, a definite emphasis on strategy. The team wants to strike the right balance between brawn and savvy. The game looks deceptively simple but the language of The Ba' – the curious hand gestures; the unspoken code – plays a major part. A circling finger indicates to team-mates that they should use their strength to try and spin the pack in an effort to get some momentum going and to shift the action in the desired direction.

The Uppies were initially aiming to get the game out of Broad Street and into the mouth of the narrower Victoria Street, which would hand them a huge advantage. Likewise, the Doonies were targeting the relative tightness of Albert Street. Force the ba' out of Broad Street and into the less roomy spaces and your opponents face a harder time of it. There is also the belief that the longer the ba' remains in Broad Street the more likely it is to go doon.

I hadn't a clue where the ba' was. There was no point in playing spot the ba'. It was in there somewhere, probably with several pairs of hands on it. Most of the Ba' players couldn't have known where the ba' was. The majority must never touch it during the course of the game. Maybe this mystery and suspense partly fuelled the fanaticism. Right now the ba' might be tucked under someone's shirt at the core of the hysteria.

The bloated pack was wedged up against the wall of the Town Hall, some on the periphery squashed up against the building. I could see how you might end up with crushed ribs. A struggling figure was hauled to safety. The man looked utterly exhausted. At least the game pauses to let a player out when they're in trouble. Medics were on stand-by just in case, but the fact is that someone will be injured. It's inevitable. There has in fact been one fatality during The Ba', back in 1903 when someone suffered a heart attack.

Suddenly the pack broke into a stampede, a wave of bad news crashing towards me. I was able to shift out of the way just in time. I'd been too close with my camera but no picture was worth that. Seasoned Ba' watchers can spot a break coming and anticipate sudden eruptions. Sensible spectators keep their distance, although some of the wives and girlfriends of the Ba' men remain at fairly close quarters, offering their support. When their man staggered from the pack, seeking some respite, a bottle of water would be thrust into his hands and he'd gulp greedily before diving back into the human whirlpool.

If anything, the Doonies appeared to be making progress, for the pack had definitely moved further down Broad Street, which actually slopes slightly in the Doonies' favour. It wasn't long though before there was another split. It happened so fast. Now there were two smaller packs and confusion abounded. Which pack had the ba'? Some of the men involved in one pack began thinking the ba' was in the other pack and dropped off to join it. Then everyone re-formed and it became one seething mass again.

Tempers started to flare, fists flew. Cooler heads – usually older heads – tried to calm down the agitated, the voices of veterans scolding younger players. Everything about The Ba' looks wrong and unlawful, but foul play is not tolerated and brawling is most certainly frowned upon. Ba' players are supposed to keep their anger in check. You don't want to be disgracing yourself. Believe it or not, there is an element of sportsmanship. Two tykes began throwing punches at each other on the edge of the pack. It was a woman who stepped in to tell them to quit. Hammering home her point, she cuffed one of the culprits on the ear. That told him.

An hour into The Ba' and the Uppies and Doonies were back at The Cross. This was going to take forever. I wondered how Clare and Brian were getting on with the standing stones. Edgar had told me the longest Ba' he'd been involved in had lasted seven hours. I was hoping for a swifter conclusion than that. The average game lasts five hours, but it has been known to run for eight. 'Get it shifted!' shouted someone. My sentiments exactly. No one was giving an inch. And still Uppies and Doonies were bumping into each other for the first time and exchanging New Year's greetings, before firing themselves back into the heat of the battle. A fatigued player stumbled from the pack to quench his thirst. 'Oh fuck,' he mouthed silently. He was feeling it.

There was excitement as a breakaway group scrambled down St Magnus Lane with others in hot pursuit. Was it a decoy or was it for real? In the end, it amounted to nothing and after the false smuggle we were back on Broad Street. At least the Doonies were holding their ground. Maybe it would be their day. But after a couple more splits, the Uppies began pulling away up Broad Street. They were turning the tide in their favour.

No one is quite sure how old The Ba' is, but it has been contested in Kirkwall for at least three centuries. Some believe it to be older than that. There are various theories concerning the origin of The Ba'. The Vikings liked it rough and – as the Norse sagas show – were partial to the occasional ball game. Then there is the gory story of a Scottish tyrant who was excecuted and his severed head was booted through the streets of Kirkwall by the people who fancied celebrating the despot's demise with an impromptu kick-about.

There is the concept of The Ba' as fertility ritual: the Doonies landing the ba' in the sea ensuring a good year's fishing and an Uppie success bringing the farmers a bumper harvest. Alternatively, The Ba' could be linked to the competing rulers of the Orkney of old, the Bishop and the Earl. The cross and the crown would often lock horns, sometimes violently. Maybe they tried to iron out their differences with The Ba'.

What is certain is that street football was once popular throughout Britain. Even today, Kirkwall isn't the only place you'll find men competing like this in the streets. There are several hand-ba' games occurring annually in the Borders, the most famous of which is the Jethart Ba', held in the town of Jedburgh every February. On the surface, it sounds very much like the Kirkwall Ba'. The Uppies and the Doonies meet at the Mercat Cross. But in other ways it is markedly different. The ba' is much smaller and is decorated with ribbons. The play is more open. The colourful back story to the Jethart Ba' is an ancient battle between the Scots and the English. The Scots, as legend has it, hacked off the heads of their enemies and kicked them through the streets of Jedburgh. The ribbons on the ba' represent the hair of the English victims. They haven't played the ba' in Jedburgh with the head of an Englishman for many a year . . . if they ever did.

More than a dozen of these ancient hand-ba' contests are still alive and kicking in Britain, some relying on just a small number of enthusiasts. There are games in England, from Cumberland to Cornwall, though the Kirkwall Ba' surely takes some beating, and not just literally. Some of the games have fallen by the wayside. There was once a game in Foulden, in the Borders, where the villagers pitted themselves against the country folk. The ball was thrown-up halfway between the church and the mill and one of the goals was the pulpit. At Scone, in Perthshire, the annual custom was for the married men and bachelors to take each other on until sunset. The husbands had to drop the ball in a hole in the moor while the singletons meant to dip it in the river. In the event of a deadlock, the ball was cut to pieces. A similar game took place in the Borders village of Coldingham where the married men had to soak the ball in the sea and the bachelors had to hit a barn door. Maybe that's where the phrase 'he couldn't hit a barn door' comes from?

At Monymusk, in Aberdeenshire, they played at Christmas, just like in Kirkwall. A minister of the time gives a good account of the ba' mania, once you get past the Doric.

The hurry-burry now began,
Was right weel worth the seeing,
Wi' routs and raps frae man to man
Some getting and some gieing.

And a' the tricks o' fut and hand,
That ever was in being,
Sometimes the ba' a yirdlins ran,
Sometimes in air was fleeing,

Sae mony weel-beft skins,
Of a' the ba'men there was nane
But had twa bloody shins,
Wi' strenzied shutters many ane.

I gather someone got kicked in the shins.

The Uppies were on the brink of Victoria Street. It was approaching three o' clock. They'd been at it for two hours. The pack was up against the phone box. How many Uppies and Doonies can you fit in a phone box? Only one of each – they're big bastards. It was a good job there wasn't anyone on the phone. Mind you, who uses phone boxes these days? 'There's Doonies on either side, no danger of us getting it out,' cried one Uppie to another. They were boxed in a corner. They wanted Victoria Street. Eventually, with a ridiculous amount of effort, the Uppies got the pack to where they wanted it. The ba' never went back down the street after that.

Occasionally The Ba' has been played indoors. Not because of bad weather, but because sometimes the ba' has actually ended up indoors. And you didn't want to be the owner of that property. Once, the manse was invaded and roundly trashed by Uppies and Doonies. They didn't care about the ornaments on the sideboard; they were just after their ba'. I once had a poster of Zinedine Zidane. There was a quote from Zidane on it. 'Sometimes the only way in is through.' I dismissed it as havering from Zidane but it turns out he was talking about The Ba'.

In the rich history of The Ba', there has been The Ba' on ice, The Ba' in the mud, The Ba' cross-country, The Ba' in a hotel kitchen, The Ba' in a coal cellar. The Ba' has an eventful past. Horse-play has been involved, quite literally. Then there is the strange case of the ba' being hidden behind a cow. One year some Uppies tumbled into a car and drove up the road with the ba'. The Doonies once resorted to a rowing boat. The ba' has been buried in the sand at low tide (I suspect the Uppies of that) and players and spectators have been known to end up in the harbour. Other times, the knives have been out. Once, when the Doonies knew they were beaten, they slashed the ba' to pieces. Then there was the time a second ba' materialised, causing all manner of confusion. Injuries have even been faked in desperate attempts to alter the course of the game.

The winter night was upon us. The street lights cast an orange glow over these Orcadian manoeuvres in the dark. The temperature had dropped but, at the heart of the pack, the energy never dipped. The Uppie juggernaut showed no sign of relenting. Doonies were dropping off and darting down lanes to tackle the pack (which spread the width of Victoria Street) from another angle. 'If it keeps going up,' sighed a spectator, 'that'll kill it.' The Doonies had to do something. It wasn't through a lack of trying – God knows, they were trying – but they needed that spark of inspiration. They required something special . . . like a successful smuggle. This remained the single biggest threat to the Uppies and was perhaps the Doonies' only hope. A few Doonies sprang from the pack and sped off as if they had the ba' but the hoax was realised instantly. No one was buying it. The pack split in two again, creating another one of those conundrums. Who had the ba'? 'Your ba' is over here,' called someone.

Did he know something or was he bluffing? Soon it was one tumultuous throng again, the pack backed into another corner, this one next to the Orkney Hotel. Tactics were discussed, encouragement was shouted and rumours spread like wildfire. Bedraggled players left the pack, coughing and groaning. A few were dragged out (before they passed out) and handed over to loved ones. One Ba' man paused from playing, cool as you like, and rolled a fag. He took a few puffs before returning to the fray. Hotel guests looked down from their bedroom windows. They were afforded an aerial view of The Ba'. One man glanced down and then turned away, as if this type of thing always happened outside his hotel window.

The Uppies were eager to get the ba' out of this corner and further up the street. Repeated attempts were made to budge the pack. The Doonies seemed happy for it to remain where it was, but the Uppies weren't having it. 'One, two, three, heave boys!' bawled an Uppie. 'Come on, get in there. Go-go-go.' And, with that, the Uppies got the game back on track. 'It's inevitable now,' commented one watcher. The pack settled once more on Victoria Street and then an unexpected thing happened. The ba', which had been buried since the throw-up a few hours ago, suddenly spilled into the air above the heads of the Uppies and Doonies. There was the briefest of glimpses of the prize and there was pandemonium as both teams jostled to catch it. The ba' was devoured by the mob and the shock of seeing it passed.

It looked like the pack was going nowhere fast, so I gambled on a pint. I ducked under the plank that blocked the door of the Orkney Hotel bar (well, you can't have The Ba' in the pub) and found quite a scene. The place was jumping. I pushed my way to the bar. I looked up and saw the blackboard on the wall. Uppies 3 Doonies 0. They were keeping the score. It was looking like a whitewash. I sat down and got talking to a bloke who, I have to say, was a bit sozzled, but it was New Year after all. He made the point that while The Ba' is a boisterous affair, no one is ever arrested. I should hope not too. He then focused on the current plight of the Doonies and thought how they could dig themselves out of a hole. 'They'll try to smuggle it at night. It's their best chance . . . any dirty trick in the book.' I left the man and minded my head on my way out of the pub.

Before I caught up with the pack – they hadn't gone too far – I popped into a shop doing a brisk trade in mince rolls. The smell had lured me in the door and I wasn't disappointed with my first ever mince roll. I grew up on my mam's and my Granny Stewart's mince and tatties but never had I encountered mince in a roll. It's a messy business alright but my goodness it was tasty and just what I needed. I licked the last of the mince off my fingers and chased after the pack, while making sure not to run into them. I kept a safe and respectful distance, at the same time regretting not buying a second mince roll.

The Ba' was nearing its endgame. The pack rumbled from Victoria Street onto Main Street and the Uppies were almost home. The Doonies desperately tried to change the script but the Uppies were being obstinate in their quest for yet another victory. The rain was falling heavily but Mackison's Corner was in sight. Only the undying determination of the Doonies was keeping this game alive. But it was in its death throes. The Uppies reached the gable end at five o'clock. They just had to knock the ba' off that wall, but it was easier said than done. The Doonies' stubborn resistance postponed the inevitable. The ba' surfaced in the hands of an Uppie but he was driven back down into the pack. Up he came again. He tried to throw the ba' off the wall but the throw fell short and the ba' sank into the angry sea of Uppies and Doonies. The crowd roared for both sides. Finally an Uppie – he turned out to be Stephen Kemp – raised himself above the rest and bounced the ba' off the gable end. Cameras flashed and loud cheers filled the cold night air. Four and a half hours after the throw-up, the Uppies had finished the job. The Doonies didn't hang about. They sloped off in their droves, leaving the Uppies to celebrate. Except that it wasn't quite over yet . . .

The Uppies had to decide who the ba' winner was. They began arguing among themselves and this – even though I'd been aware it would happen – was the most bizarre aspect of what had already been a surreal day. The pack was just like before, minus the Doonies. One final epic struggle had to run its course. Three or four Uppies started vying for recognition from within. They wanted their hands on that ba' and hoped that their team-mates would lift them up and honour them. This was the moment a winning team became warring individuals. The internal debate was furious, judging by the pushing and pulling. Who would win out and take the acclaim? You don't know what sort of support you'll get from your colleagues until you go looking for it.

It was all over bar the shouting. The crowd put in their penny's worth. It became incredibly noisy and fairly acrimonious. Women were going steadily hoarse with their shouting. One woman was going mental, her screams dominating the rest. 'Nipper's ba'!' she shrieked. 'Nipper's ba'!' Over and over again. 'Nipper's ba'!' Wife, girlfriend, sister, arbiter of justice, whoever she was she was making one heck of a racket. 'Nipper's ba'! Nipper's ba'!' She wanted Nipper to have the ba'. That ba' had Nipper's name on it. 'Just gie it to him, that'll shut her up,' said an exasperated man behind me. He sounded nearly at his wits' end and, as far as he was feeling, this was psychological torture.

But then a hairy would-be-hero rose from the pack and launched himself over the heads of his fellow Uppies. He was effectively crowd surfing, stretching and straining towards where the ba' seemed to be. As far as he was concerned it was his. Then someone shouted, 'Sigurd's ba'!' For it was Sigurd Gibson himself, flying through the air with not the greatest of ease. He was attempting to slide over his colleagues to reach his target. He seemed hell-bent on it. Sigurd wanted it badly. I started shouting 'Sigurd's ba'!' but was silenced by a scream of 'Nipper's ba'!' She had me beaten in the screaming stakes. No one could match her. But could Sigurd see off Nipper? The younger Gibson brother was still up there. It was a huge effort. He obviously felt a strong sense of entitlement to be extending that amount of effort. He'd proved his Uppie credentials over the years – or maybe, as I recalled Edgar's explanation of Ba' politics, Sigurd was mainly laying down a marker for future consideration as the ba' winner. Whatever his reasons, he wasn't letting up.

This election was intense. The battle was over, but the war was yet to be won. It looked like in-fighting, but the Uppies were merely sorting it out the way every winning team does. We'd gone a good half-hour of this stupendous popularity contest and there was no end in sight, although Sigurd had slipped back into the pack. 'They're taking an affa while,' said one man who perhaps needed home for his tea. And then, shortly after six o' clock, after 45 minutes of them trying to sort this out, an Uppie sat on the shoulders of those around him, clutching the ba'. It was Nipper, real name Neil Stockan. He lifted the ba' like it was the World Cup. It was more than the World Cup. Nipper was on top of the world. The spotlight was his despite Sigurd's strenuous efforts. Sigurd would have to fight another day. There was always next Christmas. I watched Edgar console Sigurd with a brotherly pat on the back. I didn't go over. I didn't want to intrude on the disappointment that had tempered the happiness of an Uppie victory.

The general consensus was that the Doonies had put up a good fight but that the Uppies had been spot on with their tactics. The Doonies hadn't made it easy but it wasn't enough to cause an upset. Yet there was renewed hope for the Doonies despite the clean sweep by the Uppies over the Christmas and New Year period. Today had seen a tremendous tussle and I was exhausted, even though I'd played no part in it. The happy Uppies were heading back to their base, the Orkney Hotel, where I'd had that pint earlier. I joined them in their celebrations. I figured Edgar and Sigurd had gone home.

But you share your victory with your team-mates and it wasn't long before the brothers walked into the bar. Sigurd asked me if I'd enjoyed it. I said I had and that I'd been rooting for him; I'd been shouting his name. Straight away, I felt stupid. Who was I to shout when I'd never been to The Ba' before? Edgar sat down and was sanguine about Sigurd's failed attempt. 'It's just one of these things. Sigurd's got plenty years ahead of him.' Edgar admitted being left with mixed feelings about the day but he stressed that though Nipper had beaten Sigurd there were no grudges. 'Sigurd and him are the best of pals,' said Edgar as he winced. 'I've got a bit of cramp in me back.' Edgar looked like he'd gone twelve rounds with the Doonies but he'd relished their strong challenge. 'That's as good a game as we've had for a number of years.'

What keeps The Ba' so alive? Well, they're a steadfast bunch up in Kirkwall. They have a strong identity and isolation probably helps. The Ba' has been preserved down the years, despite occasional attempts by the powers-that-be to ban it. The disapprovers have tried to take their ba' away, but without success. Those who would put a stop to it are crowded out by the clamour of the many who celebrate it. The Ba' has been variously described in the past as absurd, outrageous, foolish and barbarous. But this rock-hard spectacle is well supported. And it's a great social occasion occurring at the most sociable time of the year. The Ba' is the key to the festive season in Kirkwall. The people of this 6,000-strong town know full well what The Ba' is about. It's about community and roots. It's a time-honoured tradition that should be respected and fought for. You fight for yourself, you fight for your team, you fight for your friends, your ancestors and for the glory. And The Ba' will be around long into the future. There's enough passion and goodwill to keep the home fires burning. The Uppies and Doonies will continue to clash and go at it, to celebrate and commiserate.

My Orkney New Year was difficult. I had been low but I'd been picked up by The Ba', the toughest gig I'd have all year. My second assignment, in ten days' time, would be closer to home. And that's about the best I could say about it – because I was heading to The Broch.

Apocalypse Noo

– The Clavie, Burghead –

Och, not The Broch. I can't believe I'm writing about The Broch. I suppose with this being a book about Scottish festivals and all that, it's unavoidable. But *The Broch*?

For the uninitiated – and untainted – among you, The Broch is the village (of the damned) of Burghead on the otherwise glorious Moray Firth. The Broch is a godforsaken place. It's the Forbidden Midden. To venture into The Broch is to enter the very Heart of Darkness. It's like turning to the Dark Side. It's what I had to do to bring you this chapter. I hope you're happy. If you're not happy, then I suggest you take a running jump into The Broch.

Two miles from The Broch is my hometown of Hopeman. Two miles aren't nearly enough. The main problem with The Broch is that it's full of Brochers. I can't quite put my finger on what's wrong with them; they're just wrong. They're kind of funny-looking and have strange habits. The Clavie is one of them. More of that in a minute.

Hopemaners (that's the fine, upstanding people of Hopeman, like myself) and Brochers don't mix. We don't really like them and they don't really like us. This mutual disrespect suits us fine. We call them Brochers, with a practised roll of the eyes and a perfect grimace. They call us Cavers. This has something to do with us having roofs over our heads.

The Broch's jealousy towards Hopeman is almost overwhelming. I guess they can't help being Brochers. It's their fate. Life dealt them a bad hand and they can only make the worst of it.

Here's a neat illustration of the ill-feeling between Hope-maners and Brochers. Hopeman FC has its own Bebo page where you can read lots of wonderful stories about Hopeman FC, such as that they won the European Cup in 1974. On the Hopeman FC Bebo page, this is what's listed under Hate:

Brochers.

Nothing more needs to be said.

I remember playing football for Hopeman against The Broch many moons ago. We held our noses and entered the Forbidden Midden and thrashed the Brochers 22–1 on their own patch of dirt. I'm not even sure they scored one, come to think of it. Our dream strike partnership of Kevvy 'Hot Shot Hamish' Bruce and Marky 'McCoist' Stewart tore the Brochers to pieces. Kev scored at least ten that day and Marky helped himself to a couple of hat-tricks. Craig Fiske and Lorne Davidson marshalled the midfield and Mark Fennell bossed the defence. Stevie Murray dazzled on the left wing and I hogged the right wing where my team-mates never bothered to pass the ball. But, oh, it was great being a part of it. Hopeman showed no mercy and quite right too. They were Brochers in need of a good beating. And who better to dish it out than the Hopeman All-Star XI? Or Hope-man All-Star X plus me.

A few years ago a Hopeman–Burghead fixture turned nasty. It wasn't the players' fault. The 'fans' were to blame. My little brother played in the game. Or at least Stewart tried to play as empty beer bottles flew over his head. He spent much of the match ducking. It was shocking stuff and not surprisingly the match was abandoned. In the build-up to the carnage, there had been the usual foul-mouthed behaviour associated with the derby, the easy trading of insults ('You can stick your fucking Clavie up your arse', that sort of thing), but the flashpoint for the violence, the single provocative act that lit the blue touchpaper, was when the Brochers produced an effigy of the Black Sheddy and proceeded to set it on fire in front of the outraged home support. The Black Sheddy, if you haven't heard of it, is a shed beside Hopeman harbour. It's not even black, but it's where the wise men of Hopeman have congregated for centuries to debate the important matters of the day. The Black Sheddy is Hopeman's parliament. My Granda Sutherland had a seat in the Black Sheddy. And now the Brochers were torching it, acting all Guy Fawkes. It was disgraceful behaviour and the Hopeman fans were livid. No wonder there was a riot.

Brochers.

In all my years as a proud Hopemaner, I had never been to the Burning of the Clavie, mainly because it was a festival that occurred in Burghead. I'd always assumed you didn't go if you were from Hopeman. The Burning of the Clavie was a Broch thing. Let them keep their weird winter fire festival to themselves. So what if it was Pictish? It was rubbish.

But now I had to go to the bloody thing for this book.

I suppose I'd better tell you what the Clavie is all about and why the Brochers make such a big deal of it. You know, they never stop going on about their precious Clavie. It's Clavie this and Clavie that. Clavie, Clavie, Clavie, Clavie. Honest to God, I was sick of it. And I hadn't even been yet.

On 11 January every year without fail – unless the 11th falls on the Sunday, in which case the Clavie goes ahead on the 10th – the daft Brochers carry their big barrel of burning tar, the Clavie, around the mean streets of The Broch until the Clavie reaches its final resting place on top of Doorie Hill where more fuel is added to the fire until the Clavie breaks up and eager Brochers scramble to pick up a precious piece of their Clavie as if it will bring them good luck in the coming year – when really it's all just a piece of superstitious nonsense.

And that's how they celebrate New Year in The Broch. They ignore Hogmanay and wait till the 11th of January – just to be weird. When the old Julian calendar was replaced by the Gregorian calendar in 1752, not everybody followed suit. The Brochers were a bit slow on the uptake and carried on celebrating Old Yule Night on the 11th of January. You'd think they might have seen sense by now and stepped into line with the rest of the country, but no, they're still at it. The Brochers are a thrawn bunch . . . and that's tantamount to a compliment.

The pig-headed Brochers have been burning their Clavie for hundreds of years and, at long last, someone from Hopeman has the opportunity to put in print what Hopemaners have always thought about the Clavie. I could just type the words BAN THE CLAVIE (in upper case letters for added emphasis) but then that wouldn't be fair, would it? I hadn't been to the Burning of the Clavie yet. Objectivity and all that. I decided to give it a chance.

The fire festivals of Old Yule once blazed throughout the north, but only the Brochers were bloody-minded enough to keep theirs going. The Clavie has survived down the years through sheer stubbornness, the Brochers adamant that their blessed Clavie should endure so that they could continue to harp on about it while your average Hopemaner (not that we're average; in every way we're superior) sniggered at the silliness of it all. The Brochers go on about the importance of the Clavie and how unique it is, but, to a Hopemaner, that doesn't make it right. Still, best leave them to it.

Clavie rhymes with gravy and you must be of good stock (apologies for that) to have a whiff of a chance of being a member of the Clavie Crew. It is considered the highest honour for a Brocher to be asked to carry the Clavie. In charge of the Clavie Crew (now don't laugh) is the Clavie King. He's the master of fire ceremonies, the modern Prometheus. More on him soon. (He's quite a character.)

The basis of the Clavie is a specially modified barrel nailed to a pole. The same nail is used every year, because the Brochers don't have another one. The nail isn't knocked in with a hammer. Nope, that would be too normal. It's bashed in with a stone . . . a stone from the throne of the Pictish Kings. And if you believe that, you're a Brocher. Staves are fixed between the bottom of the barrel and the post to stabilise the Clavie. The Clavie is filled with pieces of wood daubed in tar. Finally the Clavie is lit with a burning bit of peat because using a match or lighter would be too simple.

Brochers.

(Rolled eyes, perfect grimace.)

The word Clavie is a puzzle. It could come from *cliabh*, the Gaelic word for basket. Others have said it's from the Latin *clavus*, meaning nail. Beyond the meaning of the word, there's the whole mystery of what the Burning of the Clavie signifies, other than the fact that the people of Burghead have always been off their heads. The Clavie may have been about warding off evil spirits and bringing good fortune to this close fishing community. Or it could have been simply about welcoming the longer days since the northern winter is dominated by darkness. Come to think of it, the sun hardly ever shines in Burghead. Many a summer's evening I've stood on the beach at Hopeman bathed in sunshine and glanced along the coast to find Burghead stuck under a giant black cloud. It can look similar to the sky over Mordor.

It was the big day in The Broch, the day of the Clavie, and there was an entire – and unwarranted – page devoted to it in the local paper, the otherwise excellent *Northern Scot*. I read the interview with the Clavie King. This would be Dan Ralph's twentieth year in the, ahem, hot seat and his forty-third year with the Clavie Crew. In his interview, Dan highlighted The Broch's strong identity and boasted that the Clavie could never be stopped, not even if there was a tornado. It was typical Brocher talk. 'Brochers,' I muttered. I rolled my eyes and made a perfect grimace. Next to the interview with the Clavie King was a poem entitled 'The Broch's New Year'. It was nothing but a piece of Broch propaganda. Reluctantly, I share it with you.

THE BROCH'S NEW YEAR

Whar's the year gone tae? I dinna ken at a'
It seems jist lik' yesterday, we gethered at the wa'
Tae renew The Broch's connection, wi' oor ancient ancestrie
An' think o' Picts an' Vikings, an' the things they eased tae dee.

I think o' the crew that kept me richt, when I wis jist a loon
The Rosses, Ralphs and McKenzies when Peep he wore the croon
When Jack Ross cried 'Hip Hip Hooray' the hale toon jined his cheer
For this wis The Broch – they wir the crew an this wis their New Year.

Bit noo the crew's sair made wi' threats, an' vile bureaucracee
Wi bobbies layin doon the law – as bobbies tend tae dee
Crowd control, they're spikin o' – wi' threats o' litigation
Keep a'body aff the Doorie Hill! – jist picture the sensation.

Throw less creosote! Cut doon the fire!
There's naebody stanin' here!
Awa ye go an' lave's alane
For this is oor New Year.

Bit b'guided by the stewards, as ye dodge the sparks an' flame
Dinna venture ower close – an' lave yer dogs at hame
An' when wi reach The Doorie Hill jine in wi' a' the throng
An' cheer tae gee's encouragement – it fairly spurs us on.

The Clavie it's eternal – endurin' throu' the years
We're nae pit aff b'bureaucrats, wi' a' their doots an' fears,
We've weathered mony a storm an' gale, we'll weather plenty mair,
For this is The Broch! An' we're the crew! An' this is oor New Year!

Don't worry if you don't speak Broch. It's essentially Hope-manese spoken badly. So I'll translate. The gist of The Broch's New Year is this:

'We're brilliant and don't tell us what to do, okay?'

Brochers.

(Rolled eyes, perfect grimace.)

I was on my way to The Broch with a heavy heart and a long face. My friend Jonathan had decided to join me (you know, strength in numbers). Jonathan is into the Picts. He has more than one book about them. We were in Pict country right enough. Burghead was once the capital of the Pictish Kingdom (I'll give them that). But I warned Jonathan that he wouldn't be into Brochers; that he'd probably find them quite repellent. Jonathan said he'd reserve judgement until he'd actually met some. He also argued that my opinion of Brochers was invalid because it was biased. I pointed out to Jonathan that my view was the truth. 'Let it go Gary, let it go,' said Jonathan in a mock-soothing manner. 'Let's not go,' I suggested. Jonathan brought up the fact that I was the one writing a book about Scottish festivals. I admitted to that. But then he really riled me by saying: 'You're all Picts anyway. Gary, you're practically a Brocher.' This touched a nerve.

You see, the thing is, Jonathan wasn't far off the truth. All of my Broch-baiting falls down when I face up to the facts and make the difficult admission that I'm, um, part-Brocher. The day it dawned on me I cried 'NnnnnoooooOOOO!' like Luke Skywalker when he found out Darth Vader was his real father. My father was my real father and he wasn't Darth Vader either, but he was bona-fide half-Brocher.

My dad's mam, my Granny Sutherland, was a Brocher. And she married a great man from Hopeman, my Granda. My dad and his three sisters were brought up in Hopeman, but there was Broch in them, because of their mam – and so there's Broch in me. Now you might think, 'What's he on about?' And sure, it's nothing like being, say, French-Chinese or Scots-Italian. But it means something if you're from Hopeman and part-Brocher. Where you come from helps define you. I'm Scottish, but I'm a Hopemaner. And a bit of a Brocher to boot.

Jonathan found this funny. 'Going to The Broch to see your Broch cousins.' 'Very funny, Jonathan.' 'Your Broch brothers and sisters.' 'Give it a rest, will you?' 'Heading back to your roots.' I'd had enough of Jonathan and we were only halfway to The Broch. We were walking along the disused railway line between Hopeman and the Dark Side. When I was little, I used to pick brambles off these bushes with my Granny Stewart. It's a lovely walk along the old railway line with the magnificence of the Moray Firth on one side. At least the first part of the walk is lovely. The closer you get to The Broch the more depressing and overcast it gets. With idyllic Hopeman falling away behind you, you're faced with the looming grey monolith of the maltings on the outskirts of The Broch. It's quite an introduction to the Forbidden Midden and, in its own offensive way, it's the perfect introduction.

But it had to be said that Jonathan and I were privileged because we had been invited to the court of the Clavie King. I'd phoned Dan a couple of days before and his wife had answered. Dan wasn't in but Katie said we should just pop round on Clavie night; that they'd have a houseful, but we'd be more than welcome. She said I had good connections, meaning that I had some Broch in me. Coming to the house would be good for me, she said, because the Clavie Crew would be there and I'd get a proper sense of it all. In other words, I'd get hassle. There may be Broch in my bones, but essentially I was a Hopemaner entering the lion's den.

I rang Dan's doorbell and we were welcomed in. Just about the first person I saw was my friend Nayland. He was there with his mam, Margaret, and his girlfriend, Laura. I've known Nayland since school. Like me, Nayland lives in Glasgow. Nayland is the acceptable face of the Broch and I like him a lot. A few months beforehand, we had shared a memorable night in Glasgow. A few of us were in the State Bar, my favourite pub in the city. It was me, Nayland, Clare, Steve (fellow Hopemaner), my mam and my dad. We were watching Scotland play France in Paris, in a qualifier for the European Championships. It was the night James McFadden scored the goal we never imagined a Scottish player could score and a nation went nuts. I'll never forget watching the last half-hour of that game; the nervous excitement, the giddy disbelief, the fear of waking up and discovering it was all a dream, the fear of France scoring. I picture Nayland and Steve drinking dram after dram, my dad laughing, Clare smiling, my mam shaking her head at the silliness of it all. We were in it together, staring at each other, shrugging at strangers, wondering if it was even possible that the final whistle would sound and Scotland would have beaten France. When I want a recent good memory of my dad, I think of that night and Nayland was part of it. We'll never forget it and we'll always remind each other of it. Nayland was very young when he lost his dad. Maybe that's why I felt able to talk to him about my loss. He was always Steve's friend more than mine. They were the guys in a band together. But, as the years have gone by, and we've grown older, I've grown to love the little guy. Nayland's tiny, and he won't mind me saying so. His nickname at school was Smurf. But he's got a big heart and you won't meet a nicer guy. And yet he's a Brocher.

The kitchen was packed. There were men in boiler suits and

donkey jackets, stout boots and woollen hats: The Clavie Crew. Friends and family were in attendance too and there was an amazing spread of food. There was whisky too, and laughter. In short, there was a wonderful atmosphere in the room. The conversation flowed and the drams went down smoothly. I did feel though as if there was a sign over my head that said 'recently bereaved'. Everyone in Burghead knew my dad. I was his son. But I was enjoying myself among familiar faces. Dan's son Danny came over to me and said hello. I braced myself. He said that his dad must have forgotten to switch on the alarm. 'It's the only explanation for there being a Hopemaner in the hoose.' I was willing to be the butt of his joke. It was good to see him. I'd known Danny for years – and his sister Ruth – but it had been a long time. Danny's in the Clavie Crew, as is his brother Lachie. They'd take their lead from their dad tonight. As I had done some weeks back.

Dan Ralph isn't just the Clavie King; he's the local undertaker. When my dad died, it was Dan our family turned to. He arranged the funeral, but to me he did more than that. In small communities, like Hopeman and Burghead, you all sort of know each other. I'd always liked Dan and he has a good swipe of my dad. My sister thinks so too. Dan and my dad could have been brothers. It's in the beard, the short stature, the big personality, the glint in the eye that hints at mischief, the way with words, and people, the sense of humour and the love of life.

And not long ago, Dan had stood in our living room in Hopeman as we tried to come to terms with our loss. There was the shock of death, the first sight of Dan in the black of his undertaker uniform, but, at the same time, the strange comfort of seeing him. His presence was reassuring, his concern genuine. He knew my dad well. And I think he was hurting too. They'd been pals. In those difficult days leading up to the day of the funeral, I was regularly on the phone to Dan, acting on behalf of the family, askinq questions, needing his help. His calmness rubbed off on me. The situation was far from okay, but Dan made me stronger. And I knew he was looking after my dad, his friend.

To go from mourning my dad to watching the Clavie in the space of a few weeks, with Dan the undertaker and then Dan the Clavie King, well, it was just the way it was. And I was glad to be a guest in his home. He was far too busy to talk to just then. He was the Clavie King after all. He had a barrel to burn. But I'd get a proper chat with him later.

I spoke to Ian, one of the Clavie Crew. Ian is married to my uncle's sister. 'I'd shak yer hand, but it's covered in diesel,' smiled Ian, who was looking forward to another Clavie night, but wished the night wasn't so calm. 'It'd be better if there wis a bit mair wind.' The Clavie Crew don't want it to be too gusty, but a bit of a swirl makes the spectacle more spectacular. I was told about the night of the Clavie Gale back in 2005 when a windspeed of 120 miles per hour was recorded in nearby Kinloss. Despite the troublesome conditions they still burned the Clavie. As Dan had said in the paper, not even a tornado would dissuade the Brochers from burning their Clavie.

I'd have liked to linger in the warmth of the kitchen a little longer but it was after half past five and the burning hour was approaching. Everyone started spilling out of Dan's house and into the street where a large crowd had already gathered. You could sense the excitement among the Brochers and those visitors who had travelled to be here to witness something special. Not that I spotted any Hopeman faces in the crowd. I was the only one by the looks of it. Most Hopemaners would be back in Hopeman ignoring the fact that it was Clavie night. In the bustle, Jonathan and I got separated. A few minutes later my phone rang. 'Where are you?' asked Jonathan. I checked my bearings and explained. 'I'm next to a drainpipe, wearing a hat.' An accurate description that was greeted with hilarity at the other end and a frankly unneccessary blend of sarcasm and mockery. 'You're next to a drainpipe, wearing a hat. Thanks Gary, that's useful. Everyone's wearing a hat. Which drainpipe are you standing next to?' I didn't give him the pleasure of an answer. Ach, I'd catch up with him later.

Everyone had gathered at the Auld Manse Dyke on Granary Street where the Clavie is traditionally lit. Now here was a thing. My granny grew up in the house behind that wall. She left that house on her wedding day to marry my Granda. The ritual of the Clavie and my family history were intertwined. This wall, this dyke, had as much relevance to me as anyone else. Later on, my granny's twin brother, my Uncle Ake, built a house further along Granary Street and lived there for many years. It's the Broch house that I remember from when I was a child. (That and the house on Grant Street belonging to Dolly Lucas, my old piano teacher.)

Granny Sutherland lived with Ake after my granda died. It was a memorable experience visiting Granny and Ake as a boy. I'd walk into the front lobby and to the left was my granny's living room. It was warm and cosy, everything you'd expect of a granny's living room. I remember she had the fishermen's version of 'The Lord is My Shepherd' framed above her fire. My granda had been captain of *The Onward*.

Across the lobby from my granny's living room was Ake's living room, even though they shared the same house. The arrangement suited them both. Entering Ake's living room was something else. At first, you couldn't tell if he was in there or not due to the impenetrable fog caused by his forty-a-day Woodbine habit. I'd stumble tentatively towards the couch and just about make out the hunched figure of Ake in his chair in the corner.

He terrified me. Ake had spent much of his life at sea. He'd seen the world. Ake was a whaler, straight out of *Moby Dick*. He'd have made a better fist of catching that whale than Captain

Ahab did. It was always the same when I went to the house on Granary Street. I'd spend some time with my granny and then, just as I was about to leave, she'd say, 'Go and see your Uncle Ake.' I'd gulp and do as I was told, even though I dreaded it. I'd find Ake through the cigarette haar and he'd bark at me for a bit and then I'd say, 'See you later, Uncle Ake,' and I'd be out the door. I remember my dad used to bring jars of potted heid which Ake would scoff at the little table in his living room. I also seem to recall Ake devouring a fish in one go with his hands. He stripped the meat and then swallowed the bones, like in a cartoon. He was some man, my Uncle Ake. To a little boy, he was intimidating, but I don't think he meant to be. He was just Uncle Ake. My dad understood him. I just hid behind my dad.

When I was made Dux of Lossie High, my mam said I should tell my Granny Sutherland. So I got on my bike and cycled to The Broch on a beautiful day. After I'd surprised my granny and told her my news – she was delighted – she said, 'Go and tell your Uncle Ake.' I supposed I had to. He wasn't in his living room. He was out in the back garden, busy with his vegetable patch. He didn't notice I was there. I took a few nervous steps towards him and said, 'Uncle Ake.' He turned round and I told him my good news. For some reason, I had thought he wouldn't care. 'Well done,' said my Uncle Ake. He looked really pleased.

It was Clavie time. I couldn't wait, which was worrying (and not very Hopeman at all). The Clavie King appeared on the dyke with his burning sod of peat and popped it into the Clavie. We had fire. It lit up the faces of the Clavie Crew who were about to take turns in carrying this burning barrel round the village. There were three rounds of 'hip hip hooray' between the Clavie King and the worked-up crowd as creosote was poured on the Clavie and the flames danced higher. Some of the crew members would have had singed eyebrows already. More staves were packed into the Clavie and it was brought down from the dyke so that the procession could begin. Wives in fluorescent coats acted as stewards to keep the eager crowd at a safe distance. You didn't want to get too close to the Clavie. At best, you would ruin your coat. You wear old clothes on Clavie night. I didn't have any other kind of clothes.

Each member of the Clavie Crew would bear the considerable burden of the Clavie for a few paces before putting it down and letting someone else have a go. The carries were short and the changeovers frequent. At most, they were lifting it a foot off the ground. It's heavy work and fiercely hot. The smoke makes the eyes water and catches the throat. The Clavie carrier is left with a stiff neck and sore shoulders for a few days, but that's no great hardship when you've had the honour of carrying the Clavie.

They don't hang about either. The Crew moves at pace. It was like a sponsored speed walk with a flaming barrel in tow. I found it remarkable how quickly they were getting around the village but there is probably no point in prolonging what is already a formidable challenge for the Crew. I was struggling to keep up and all I was carrying was a camera. You could feel the intensity of the heat from 20 feet away. They weaved their way through the old streets of The Broch on a predetermined route. Sparks flew and the Crew stopped from time to time so charred staves could be broken off and offered to households as tokens of good luck for the coming year. The first stop was one of the pubs where the landlord gratefully received his piece of the Clavie.

Then we were moving down towards the harbour with the crescent moon shining over Burghead Bay and more stars in the sky than you ever see in the city. There were more hip-hip-hoorays and further words of encouragement for the Clavie Crew. Cinders on the road looked like orange stars as I trod on them. The Clavie was like the Olympic torch, except that it never left The Broch. It felt like an event that had been going on for hundreds of years. It suited The Broch. I appreciated the no-frills nature of it. Simply light the Clavie and walk. No pipe bands or anything like that. The Crew – and the crowd – raced down Dunbar Street, along King Street and then Church Street, where more pieces of the Clavie were removed and presented to residents. There was laughter as the Clavie King announced, 'There's one for The Broch's aulest man.' On one street corner, a man stamped on his smoking stave before gingerly picking it up. 'Jeeze, I'm choked,' he said with an exagerrated cough as he brought his smouldering prize into the house. Another man poured water over his piece of the Clavie before going too near it. The crowd was loving this.

The Burning of the Clavie wasn't always this popular. In past centuries, the church found it hard to tolerate and wanted it outlawed. It was damned by the Presbyterians, who considered the practice 'sinful and heathenish'. The Clavie was banned in 1704, but that didn't stop it. You can tell these Brochers what to do, but they won't listen. Old habits die hard, especially in close-knit fishing communities like this. They weren't so much die-hards as never-dies. I was beginning to admire the Brochers – something I'd never have admitted to up until now.

It was time to feed the beast, to replenish the Clavie with more staves. Dan, with his big red gloves, filled up the smoke-belching barrel. It looked like he was conducting the flames and making them dance to his tune. He was commanding fire. Dan lobbed in more bits of wood. The man was impervious to the heat. He was invincible. He was the Clavie King. Now he was emptying in a sack of something. Maybe it was kittens. You never know with Brochers. 'Watch yersels, boys,' warned Dan as he poured in some gloop from a silver pail, to loud cheers. 'Same again, boys, watch yersel,' repeated Dan as he dealt with another pail and the flames scaled new heights. Then the Crew were on the move again and we walked towards the red dots in the night sky, the lights of the giant radio masts I'd known all my life.

I'd seen some crazy things in my life. I'd done some daft things in my life. But never had I known anything like the Clavie. I felt stupid to be watching it for the first time when all the time it had been on my doorstep. The Clavie Crew turned down a lane near the top of Grant Street. 'That wifie'll need tae wash her windaes the morn,' said a man in the crowd. We were nearing Doorie Hill and the fiery finale. The Clavie was carried to the top and wedged into a pillar known as the Clavie Stone, put there a long time ago for the purpose of receiving the Clavie. More staves were chucked in and more fuel was piled on in the shape of tar and creosote. The crowd cheered as the Clavie Crew upped the ante. The Clavie was now a beacon burning bright along the coast. It was a truly spectacular sight. A little girl asked her mother 'Is there somebody in it?' Somebody in the Clavie? What had she been watching, *The Wickerman*? But all she was seeing was the confidence of the Clavie Crew as they seemingly walked through flames on Doorie Hill. I saw Danny pick up a bit of the Clavie and throw it down the hill to the delight of the nearest Brocher.

The raging Clavie was now tilted at an angle but one girl was distinctly unimpressed. 'All we're watching is fire,' she complained. She refused to join in with the next lot of hip-hip-hoorays. The Crew heaped on yet more creosote. One of them in silhouette bore a striking resemblance to Van Morrison. It was the hat. The Clavie seemed to have a life of its own now as it fizzed like a rocket about to shoot off into the sky over the Moray Firth. We stood on the site of what was once a major Pictish fort. Carved slabs with striking depictions of bulls were discovered here. One of the Burghead Bulls is displayed in the National Museum of Scotland in Edinburgh. Burghead had history, *really old* history. You know, it had a lot going for it.

I could feel the heat on my face and I wasn't even standing that close to the furnace. It was as if the whole of Doorie Hill was ablaze now. The flames were frightening. I couldn't believe the Clavie Crew were still up there, but they were clearly skilled at dodging the flames. They gave the distinct impression they knew what they were doing and what the Clavie would do next. In old times the Clavie was left to burn all night. But tonight, finally, the crumbling Clavie collapsed. There was a flow of lava down Doorie Hill. The hill is left in a blackened state but it will recover in the coming months. It can take it. The Crew moved in swiftly and broke up the remains of the Clavie, distributing pieces to the crowd and sparking a scramble for the burning embers of good luck, a clamour for a chunk of the Clavie to be carried home and kept until next year or posted abroad to family or friends. Fishermen have sneaked bits of the Clavie on board their boats for good fortune. The local MSP kept a bit of the Clavie in his office in the Scottish Parliament. Naturally it would be a lifetime of bad luck for anyone from Hopeman taking a piece of the Clavie home with them.

Now for the pub. I caught up with Jonathan. He'd enjoyed it. I'd enjoyed it. My brother had come along in the end with his girlfriend, Adele, and they'd enjoyed it. What on earth was going on? Hopemaners having a good time in The Broch? At the Clavie? We had a couple of drinks and a few of the Clavie Crew came into the pub, including Dan's son Lachie, who looked like Clint Eastwood in his cowboy hat. I introduced myself to Lachie and he reached inside his coat and handed me a piece of the Clavie. I didn't know what to do. 'I'm from Hopeman,' I said. Lachie shrugged as if this were irrelevant. Well, he was in the Clavie Crew. He knew what he was doing. Nervously – and not without a little guilt – I put the piece of Clavie inside my jacket pocket. If one of the Clavie Crew said it was okay, it must be okay. I quickly forgot about the contents of my pocket and carried on drinking.

Then I saw Ross at the bar. Ross is a long-time member of the Clavie Crew and I know him well from school. Ross sat behind me in accounts class at Lossie High. Ross loves the Clavie. So does his little boy. When Ross dug his old Clavie gear out of the garage this year – the blackened gear he was wearing now – his son got really excited. 'Oh, Dad! What's that smell?' It was the reek of the Clavie. Ross likened it to the wonder of Christmas. 'It's like Santa,' smiled Ross. 'It's magic.' Ross looked like he'd been carrying a barrel of burning tar round the village. 'You wake up the next morning and your pillow's black with soot,' laughed Ross. 'Nothing can beat it.' All these great Brochers I was meeting. My world was turning upside down.

Jonathan and I then headed for the ceilidh at the Community Hall. They have a ceilidh whenever the Clavie lands on a Friday or Saturday. Luckily this was a Saturday and Dan had sorted it out so that we could go. Nayland was going too. We got to the door of the hall and there was Dan. He'd cleaned up from the Clavie already and was looking very smart in his tartan trews. I shook Dan's hand and he told us to go and enjoy ourselves. We entered the hall where the celeidh was in full flow. Everyone sat at tables with cerry-oots either in cool boxes or plastic bags. There were sandwiches and crisps. The mood was infectious. Jonathan and I sat with Nayland and his folks. Nayland's mam, Margaret, offered me some wine. Her partner George turned to me and smiled and said something that sticks in my mind yet. 'Ye're back among yer ane here noo.' Among my own people, the Brochers. I was more than welcome. I found that enjoying myself here was the easiest thing in the world. I only wished my dad were there too but I knew I had to stop wishing these thoughts because they didn't do me any good. But he would have loved this, he really would. He'd have been up dancing for sure.

It was up to me to have fun. I got up and danced, which was rare. Nayland's girlfriend, Laura, and I did Strip the Willow. At least it might have been Strip the Willow. Don't ask me. I sat down after that and watched Nayland tearing up the dancefloor. He was clapping and grinning. Nayland said a funny thing after that. I think it was Nayland. The beer and the wine were beginning to take their toll. 'There's a rumour going around that you might be being groomed for the Clavie.' The very idea. I'd never cope with the weight of that barrel.

Much as Jonathan and I were having a wonderful time, we agreed we should be making a start back to Hopeman. We walked back along the old railway line in the dark because we were drunk enough to think it was a good idea. Never mind, we made it. Back to civilisation, I would say, except that I've stopped taking cheap digs at The Broch. I'd had an amazing night at the Clavie and I knew for sure that I would go again.

By the time we got back to Hopeman, I was in a bad way and in a bad mood. I acted like an idiot. I was my own worst enemy and everyone else's enemy. I was argumentative, boorish and disrespectful. I don't know what came over me and I'm ashamed of myself now even thinking about it. I can blame the drink. I can blame the heightened emotions surrounding my dad's death. But in the end, it boiled down to me. I'd no one to blame but myself and the next day I suffered the hangover from hell. I deserved it. I later made some apologies which were accepted with better grace than I was entitled to. I took my sore head and went for a walk on Hopeman beach. When I was down there I felt the piece of Clavie in my pocket. I'd forgotten it was there. I won't pin the blame for my poor conduct on the piece of Clavie, but I got rid of it anyway. I guess I still had some of those old Hopeman ways and attitudes.

Looking back, I learned a lot of lessons on Clavie night. The Clavie's worth seeing. The Brochers aren't bad. Me and whisky don't mix. The main lesson I had to learn was how to be a better person. And I was working on that. I only had to look as far as my dad for a role model. And if I wanted another example of how to be a good man there was my wee brother Stewart.

When I told my mam I'd come home with a piece of the Clavie and that I'd got rid of it, her reaction surprised me.

'I mind the last time ye did that.'

'Last time I did what?'

'Took a piece o' the Clavie hame.'

'But, Mam, I've never been to the Clavie before.'

'Aye ye have.'

'When?'

'Och, I dinna ken. When ye were at school.'

'But I don't remember.'

She told me that my dad was at sea at the time. I must have gone to the Clavie with a friend's dad or an uncle or somebody. I really had no recollection of it. I must have erased it from my memory, being a Hopemaner and all. Unless my mam was mistaken. But she was adamant. My dad had phoned home from the boat and my mam told him that his son had been to the Clavie. Not only had he been to the Clavie but he'd brought a piece home with him. My dad was swift in his response and his instructions.

'Get rid o' it. Thone's bad luck. There'll be nae Clavie in my hoose when I get hame!'

And him half-Brocher too. It must have been the Hopeman in him.

My mam followed his instructions and buried the piece of Clavie in the back garden near the oil tank. And now, years later, I had panicked, as my dad had done, and disposed of another piece of Clavie.

A few nights later I was back in The Broch seeing Dan. (I didn't mention throwing away a piece of the Clavie. You couldn't confess that to the Clavie King.)

'Are ye wintin a dram, Gary? A dinna drink masel on ma own. But if there's somebody in.'

I was happy to join Dan. I sat down in the comfiest living room I've ever sat down in and Dan started talking about Clavie night and how he'd slipped in the street later on. 'I'd on leather sheen fae the dancing and this wiz efter five in the morning. It wis icy. I'd Lachie's dog in one hand. I'd a few drams.' He'd been on his way back to the hall to clean up before the cleaners got there at seven. 'I didna feel like it.' But he somehow managed it.

Ever since the Clavie, Dan's life had been hectic. He'd just had another busy night of socialising. 'Singing bothy ballads. It went doon a storm. I'm a bit o' a party animal at the minute. Got hame at half past four.'

I said how much I had enjoyed the ceilidh. 'The dance is jist when the Clavie passes at a weekend. Ootwith weekends there's folk in this hoose and other hooses. They come and go till daylight. It's hard on the hoose.'

There had been a minute's silence – announced by Dan – at the dyke shortly before the Clavie was lit. I wanted to ask him about it. 'The minute's silence is becoming the norm. Nae that we wint it. We've lost a couple of Crew members. It's jist the age we are. But there's loons, grandsons. It's fine. It keeps the enthusiasm going and I can leave this world kenning that it's nae ginna die oot. It used to be whin ye were young, it was a trial of strength. If ye like, an initiation. We haud the weight for the younger anes and their confidence will come – and it allows the auler anes a break.'

I'd thought the size of the Clavie Crew was fixed at a dozen but it turns out that's not the case. 'The numbers are nae hard and fast, but it's fairly select. You've got to have a strong family connection. And you need strong, fit people. It's pretty physical. It's a walking pace but you've a lot of things to balance. It's heavy. You have to keep moving. The enthusiasm maks ye walk quickly an a'.

'It used to be – before my day – men wid come oot their hoose and cerry it tae the next hoose for good luck. It's still like that to some extent. Some Brocher will come back and say "Are ye wintin a cerry?" and they'll cerry it ten yards. It fairly fills them wi' pride.'

I said how it had been such a calm evening but that I'd been told a bit of wind is preferred.

'Aye, you've got to think aboot the weather. There wis nae wind. I prefer a bit o wind. Ye ken where tae stand. The sparks are going in one direction and there's a cooler side tae. The worst is that swirling wind. You want continuous wind in one direction, but it clarts fowks' hooses. Last year I got a phone call fae a boy. "My house is freshly painted and covered in stains. Some tarring material. What are you going to do about it?" "Well, I wid suggest squeezy liquid and a scrubbing brush and hose it doon. Thanks for letting me know. Bye." That's what I said.

'One year nae that long ago the barrel burnt through. A hole appeared in the side o' it because the wind wis that strong. Three years ago wis the night o' the Clavie Gale. Fearsome it wis. A hundred and twenty miles an oor – extremely strong – and we're battling against it.'

Dan explained the making of the Clavie. He builds his own barrel close to the original tar barrel that was once used – the archangel barrel. Only the best will do for the Clavie as far as Dan's concerned. 'For quite a long time they used a whisky barrel, which isna the right shape. It's bellied. We went up to the Faroes to look for barrels. But we had some aul photos of Crew members stanning wi yer complete barrel and we worked oot it was three feet high and twenty-four inches in diameter with wooden hooks. We canna mak ane jist wi wooden hooks and expect it to stay thegether. It would fa' tae bits. So we use iron hooks. It looks to all intents and purposes like an archangel tar barrel. It's modelled on the archangel. I felt it was important tae go back to tradition. Since then, makin the barrel, there's mair involved than there used to be, but we keep on top of it.'

Not everyone was convinced when Dan first put forward the idea of remodelling the barrel. There were a few skeptics. ' "It'll never work." "It's never been tried." Nae faith. Thought they wid be scalded tae death. If you think it's full of biling creosote ye dinna wint it running doon yer neck. But we researched it and that's nine noo. We mak it two or three weeks before and leave it full o' water. And then, the night before the Clavie, we build the Clavie. It only takes aboot an oor. The Crew assemble it in the workshop. It's tradition. And we saw the barrel and build it. It's a wonderful shape. It hauds a lot o' weight but it's a perfect shape.'

Dan went on: 'Ye're only lifting it a few feet. Yer head's underneath and it's resting on yer shooders. It's still sair, mind. We dinna veer fae the route at a'. It wis pointed out recently that it's a clockwise route, based on the rising and setting sun. But it might be coincidence. We dinna adhere strictly. In the past, it was cerried roon the pier and bits were thrown on the boats for good luck. But a boat went on fire and they stopped that. We stop at certain hooses and pubs. The reason for that's obvious. Ye get a dram!

'There's a difficulty wi the hooses. Is it the hoose or the person? I think it must be the person. When I was a teenager, a teacher, Mrs Dick, she selt her hoose. She liked the tradition o' a bit o Clavie thrown through her lobby, which wis the traditional way it was delivered. It wisna dropped ootside. It wis thrown inside yer door. The auld hooses probably had a flagstone slate. Well, it was thrown indoors and the new fowk in her hoose heard the commotion in the street, and the door opened and a bit flung in. Ye can imagine whit they thought. We were trying to burn them oot! They accepted the explanation but the next year we placed it on a shovel.'

I was brought up the belief that it was bad luck for someone from Hopeman to go home with a piece of the Clavie. Dan shot me right down. 'That's jist jealousy fae the Hopemaners, that.' Had we just made it up? The thought had never occurred to me until now.

Dan reflected on how widespread midwinter fire festivals like the Clavie once had been in the north of Scotland.

'Tar barrels were burned widely. In the Cromarty museum – the auld courthoose – there's an extract fae the local paper. Three men were jailed ten days for burning barrels. One o' them was a Ralph . . . possibly related. It happened in a lot of places, coastal communities in particular. Since they had the barrels, and possibly it was a signal tae ither coastal communities. Ye can see the Doorie Hill fae Buckie. So if ye were burning clavies folk wid ken aboot it.'

The Clavie King had his own ideas about why The Broch kept going while other similar festivals were lost to history. 'When we changed tae the Gregorian calendar fae the Julian calendar, eleven days were lost. Eventually a'body changed tae the new calendar but the Crew stuck with the Eleventh. Maybe in other communities they toed the line and it died oot. I think that's why we've still got the Clavie. We refused tae change. Because Brochers, by their nature, are . . . maybe nae dour, but defiant, stubborn, reluctant tae change.'

Why did he think his ancestors burned the Clavie?

'There's a hale oor o' extra daylight on Clavie night. If you go by the winter equinox, you come to the Eleventh o' January exactly. An oor o' increased daylight – and if you're looking for the sun after the dark winter and hoping you're not going to be in continuous darkness, it's a reason to celebrate. A great reason to have a fire and celebrate the return o' better weather and longer days. There's lots o' good reasons. I think it widna be unreasonable to say it took its origins in Viking and Pictish times, as ye ken they were baith here. Burghead was the capital of the Pictish kingdom and Pictish navy.'

I asked how he came to be involved in the Clavie.

'My father was in the Crew, and my father's brother, my uncle Dan. And my grandfather, but he went very much to the kirk and came oot o' it at an early age. His grandfather was in it an' a'. I was in the thick o' it as a bairn. The excitement. "It's Clavie night again!" And there was always a party in oor hoose. The infamous Dr Reid was a great socialiser and pianist. He played till daylight to a packed hoose. I wis encouraged an' a'. I was discouraged from having a dram and the only night the rule was broken was Clavie night, though my mother never approved o' it.'

'Since I was eighteen, I've been in the Crew. There's a photo turned up fae 1964.' Dan went to fetch it. And there he was, a young Dan, looking as proud as anything. 'An enthusiastic loon! Ma father (ye canna see) he's under the Clavie and on top is Jock Ross, the main man o' the Clavies. I can mind he was jist loaded wi charisma. He cerried a'body along wi 'im. He had a power aboot him. "Hip-hip." Jist that presence. He died in his forties. And that's me smiling ma heart oot on the night as I light the Clavie.'

Dan told me how he came to be the Clavie King.

'There was a decision by the Crew on the first Clavie efter Peep died – he died in 1987 – and the first Clavie efter, the Crew had tae decide who wid be King and they had a vote and they voted for me – because o' ma father's connection. I keep a cool heid. I never let myself get oot o' hand. Tae be the Clavie King ye dinna wint tae be shy, and Ah've never been bothered wi shyness! You have to be outspoken when it's called for. If ye're too reserved it wid dilute it slightly and we dinna want that.'

Balancing the Clavie with health and safety can cause headaches.

'Noo there's problems wi the authorities, the council demanding insurance. But we've got that sorted oot. One o' the crew is an insurance consultant.'

And there's the police to satisfy.

' "We do have the power to stop this," said one o' the bobbies. I said, "I dinna suggest you try it. There'd be civil unrest." They'd like to tak the crowds off the Doorie Hill. It's pretty dangerous, but they see it as being mair dangerous than we believe it tae be. We've gone to a lot of bother to address it. We're a' looking for safety. The mair steps we take to reduce the danger, the less we are liable.'

Throughout its history the Clavie has been under scrutiny from certain quarters. 'The only folk who were literate in the auld days were the folk in the kirk who either ignored it or criticised it. They certainly didna support it. There's a reference in the museum in Forres to a woman in the eighteenth century condemned to wear sackcloth as punishment for tar-barrelling. They saw it as pagan and discouraged it.'

I commented on how big the crowd was on Clavie night. But, to Dan, that's almost irrelevant.

'If, for some reason, nobody came into the Broch on Clavie night, we widna care. It's for the Brochers and the crowd's secondary to whit we're dein. As long as they dinna get in the road. We dinna encourage the crowd. I wid never dream o' putting it on a website, though it is in fact on a website. It's fine tae see that fit we dee is appreciated by quite a wide area, but it's nae why we dee it. It's nae a crowd puller. It's anything but a crowd puller. We're deeing it for ourselves and if anybody comes along then fine. We're nae deeing it for tourists. Though it's fine to see some folk fae abroad. It's good in some ways to ken the wider world is taking notice of us. We dinna really need it, but ach, it disna dee any herm. It's good to stand back and look through the smoke and see there's a lot of people enjoying this.

That's rewarding. And you hear comments. "Oh whit a good Clavie." It's eyewiz the best ane!'

Dan continued: 'Some o' the Findhorn Foundation folk used to come in busloads. They were getting cerried awa. Groups o' them on the Doorie Hill haudin hands in a circle and chanting. Ah thought they were a' nae weel. They were comin in droves. I suppose they were getting a lot oot o' it. I didna mind, but there's the safety element.

'Maybe fifteen years ago these ither fowk took an interest in the Clavie. They were trying to resurrect the Beltane fires. Would the Clavie Crew come doon? So they sent a video and I vowed never to go near it. They were dressed like characters oot o' *A Midsummer Night's Dream* and dancing through flames. But I wrote to them with advice – in the face of the police – and they wrote a letter about the importance of tradition.'

Dan's current concern is with the Crew not overdoing it with all they chuck on the Clavie.

'There's a balance to be found, mair and mair. The amount o' creosote that's thrown. Is it necessary? And we try tae cut back, nae to please the police. Fifty gallon's jist stupid and another twenty gasoline and the hale hill's on fire. Creosote's a special commodity. Ye canna buy it. It's unavailable noo. We bought nearly four hundred gallons from the builder's merchant. It was becoming illegal for them so we struck a deal for a good price, cos they were faced wi getting rid of it. We're trying to ration it. I dinna ken whit we'll dae when it's gone. The water-based equivalents are'na the same. In the auld days, they didna have an abundance of anything. They couldn't afford to waste huge amounts of fuel. They only had a hundred folk roon them watching and noo there's thousands and they are a' lookin for a spectacle. But how much o' a spectacle do ye gie them? I dinna wint tae reduce it either. You have to find a balance and it's a fine balance. An it can be spectacular cos o' the wind. Every ane's different.'

I mentioned Ross's story of his son getting excited when his dad took his Clavie clothes out for Clavie night. Dan smiled. 'Aye, Ross. His loony Jamie cerried it up the close. He wiz underneath it. Ye see the pride in his face. He's a dead cert for the Crew! That's great tae ken.'

Dan's sons were always dead certs for the Clavie Crew. 'Lachie and Dan, I encouraged them from an early age. It's infectious.'

I knew full well that the Clavie eclipsed New Year in The Broch but I wanted to know how much Christmas and New Year were relegated. 'Christmas I mair or less ignore,' said Dan, pouring me another dram. 'I like to see the family but it's too commercialised for me. Hogmanay? I suppose I did celebrate it. I have a dram at the Bells but I dinna go overboard. We play it doon. There's a limit to how many times you can celebrate. You hear folk saying it's just an excuse for anither Hogmanay. To some it might be, but I dinna see it. It's the maist important time o' the whole year and it's great that it can be like that, with individuality like we have here. We have something other folk havna got. I dinna think ye'll find anything richer than the Clavie. And unchanged, mair or less. It's a great way to pass the coorsest bit o' the winter.'

At the same time, he was relieved it was over for another year. 'I'm glad to see it past and breathe a sigh of relief that naebody's hurt. We've kept the bobbies at bay. It's emotionally draining, as well as physically. I can be kind of highly strung at times, so it's a huge relief. But it's satisfying an' a', being able to do it. Being part of it's great, I jist love it. It's the maist important day in oor calendar. That and going away in the boat for two or three weeks in a year. I'm planning for Unst. Real islanders are thin on the ground.'

We talked so late I couldn't possibly phone my mam or sister in Hopeman to come and pick me up. Instead Dan's wife Katie kindly gave me a lift home.

It was only later that I realised Dan and I had talked for hours but we hadn't mentioned my dad all night. It hadn't needed to be said. And we'd been talking about the Clavie. My dad would have loved the evening I had spent, yapping to Dan. It was a damn shame, but anyway . . .

What sticks most in my mind from my conversation with Dan was him telling me his lifelong ambition: to fly over an erupting volcano. 'I'll dae it tee.' I don't doubt him. The Clavie's not hot enough for Dan.

Dan Ralph was born to be Clavie King. He's a stickler for tradition. Never mind keeping it alive; it mustn't change. Dan's a great man. Like my dad was a great man.

For the first time in my life, I went to the Clavie. And you know what?

(If you're a Hopemaner reading this, put the book down now and leave the room.)

The Clavie is an amazing thing.

Long burn the Clavie!

No. LONG BURN THE CLAVIE!

And now I can't go back to Hopeman.

From the pages of the *Northern Scot*, January 2009.
Another Clavie poem. I suspect Dan had a hand in this.

THE BROCH'S THE PLACE TAE BE

I'm richt glad I'm a Brocher, the wye that things hiv gone
The banks a' fairly let us doon, we've plenty cause tae moan
Oor economy's on a knife edge, oor jobs are on the line
The price o' a' things through the roof, oor nation's in decline.

An' yet, the Broch's the place tae be, compared wi' Lossie toon
I widna fancy bidin there – when it's twinned wi' the moon
A closer neighbour, twa miles east, has plenty cause for fricht
Balmedie's been let aff the hook, an Hopeman's in his sight.

Donald Trump his rakit up an ancient family tree
His great-granny bade in McPherson Street afore she gaed tae
    Tennessee
His latest plans come oot next week – ye'll a' collapse wi' shock
He's gyan tae build his golf resort – ower by the Daisy rock.

The Broch's the place tae be a' richt – we're lackin naething here
The price o' whisky's fair shot up – but we hae naught tae fear
Roseisle Distillery's nearly deen – an' on stream ony day
Oor pipes gyan thru the Burma Road an up the Slappy Brae.

We're self-sufficient here, ye see – in a' things man might need
Compared wi' ither Moray toons, we fairly tak the lead
Weel blessed wi' auld tradition, unique thru history
Come ower by on Clavie nicht – The BROCH'S the place tae be.

Brochers.

Burn Baby Burn, Longship Inferno

– *Up-Helly-Aa, Lerwick* –

My dad used to get stuck in Lerwick. When the waves were no longer funny and had become stupid to the point of ridiculous, *The Adonis* (INS 75) would shelter from the angry North Sea in Shetland's capital. Lerwick was a haven for Captain Sutherland and his crew. Back in Hopeman, the phone would ring in our kitchen and Mam would pick it up. When she came off the phone she'd tell her two sons: 'Your dad's in Lerwick.' We'd no idea where Lerwick was. My wee brother had little idea about anything. Stewart didn't even know that the carpet he was chewing wasn't edible. But we knew – I think even Stewart sensed it – that Dad had been having a rough time on the open seas and that was why he was in Lerwick. Such was the life of a fisherman. I never thought I'd end up in Lerwick. Not unless I became a fisherman and the weather got so bad I wound up there. But my dad wouldn't let me be a fisherman. He wanted me to do something else.

Yet here I was in Lerwick. I wasn't stuck and the weather was pretty decent given it was still January. I'd caught a flight up to Shetland by choice for a bit of boat burning. It was the last Tuesday in January which, in Lerwick, can mean only one thing: Up-Helly-Aa. I'd heard it was quite a party. I knew two other things about Up-Helly-Aa. I knew that Vikings were involved and that they torched a longship they'd gone to the bother of building. And that was about it. But I was looking forward to finding out more about Up-Helly-Aa and making a night of it.

Making a night of Up-Helly-Aa is easier done than said. The whole of Lerwick has their party helmets on.

I might as well cut to the chase. If you've never experienced Up-Helly-Aa then I suggest you get yourself to Lerwick for the last Tuesday of January. Head to Shetland and see if you can keep up with the Lerwegians. You may not manage to, but it is fun trying. Oh what a night! I'm sure I've forgotten half of it. That's what Up-Helly-Aa does to you. It's like being slapped in the face fifty times by a wet haddock. The haddock isn't slapping you in the face, and nobody slapped me in the face with a haddock, but that's what it's like. If you can't make it to Lerwick for the last Tuesday of January, I suggest you recreate Up-Helly-Aa by picking up, say, a haddock from your local fishmonger, handing said haddock to a friend and asking the friend to slap you repeatedly – say fifty times – in the face with the haddock. Then wash your face. You don't want to be stinking of fish.

On the back of The Clavie, I was off to another fiery midwinter festival, albeit one on a much larger scale. Instead of the Clavie King and his Crew, it would be the Guiser Jarl and his squad of Vikings. Plus a supporting cast of 50 other squads in costume. All told it was a thousand men. They march with their flaming torches through the streets of Lerwick, set fire to their galley and celebrate all night, gracing a dozen private parties in strict rotation and performing prepared sketches and dancing with the women. Oh and there's a bit of drinking involved. Well, can you imagine a tee-total Viking festival? I wondered if I had the stamina for it all, and I was just watching.

Shetland, like Orkney, is usually shown in a box on a map, as if it existed inside that box. Shetland shares the same latitude as southern Greenland and is not terribly far from Norway. Lerwick is closer to Bergen than Aberdeen. The name Lerwick comes from the Old Norse Leirvik, meaning muddy bay. The Vikings once dropped by Shetland and decided to stay for a while.

Up-Helly-Aa is a rousing reminder of Shetland's ancient links with the Norsemen. Britain's northernmost town was going to light up tonight. I was a long way from Glasgow, but Lerwick was party central.

I arrived at Sumburgh airport off an early-morning flight. I'd left all the bad weather back in the central belt. In Shetland, it wasn't chucking down rain for a start. Neither was it blowing a gale. It was positively mild and I could even see the sun. This wasn't my idea of Shetland in January but I wasn't knocking it. The light had a special quality too. I felt like I was part of a slightly over-exposed photograph. It was strange, but nice.

Thankfully there were no Vikings blockading the airport. But waiting for me as I entered the terminal building was Elma. She was holding a piece of white card with my name on it. I'd never had that happen to me at an airport before. It was always someone else. It made my morning. I'd never met Elma before. We'd exchanged emails after I had made some initial enquires about Up-Helly-Aa. Elma conducts guided tours on the island and she'd offered to collect me from the airport and drive me the 25 miles to Lerwick, which was very good of her.

'You'll no' be going to bed at all,' said Elma, noting my lack of luggage. She'd sorted me out with a ticket for one of the all-night hall parties. These tickets are like gold dust and it's not easy for a visitor to get a hold of one but, thanks to Elma, I had. She quite approved of my plan of not bothering with a hotel booking, since I was going to one of the halls. I'd be on the first flight back home tomorrow morning. I wasn't planning on getting any sleep at all because nobody else in Lerwick was intending on sleeping tonight (when in Rome and all that).

As Elma drove along the road past wonderful rugged scenery – a stark contrast to Orkney, which had seemed pretty flat to me, matching my mood at the time – she started telling me about Up-Helly-Aa. 'What it really is about is welcoming back the

longer days. Because we live in this dark place, we're pleased to
see the sun. After the shortest days, you're on an upward climb.
You can see half-an-oor's difference in the daylight now.'

This craving for light in the deep of winter was chiming with
the Brochers and their Clavie.

'We were great believers in the little people . . . the sub-
terranean people,' continued Elma.

I gave her a quizzical look.

'What I'm talking about is the trowels.'

Gardening?

'New Year's Eve was the night that the trowels entered the
townships. Everything had to be saved from the trowels.'

Trowels stalking the landscape? I was fairly confused. It would
be the theme of my 24 hours in Lerwick (confusion, not
trowels).

'There were various ways of doing it. For the animals, you
went into the yard and drew a straw from each stack of corn and
you braided them together and pinned them up above the byre
door. Then you laid a knife next to the door, and a Bible.
Because the trowels dusna like any kind of good words and they
don't like steel for some reason.'

It dawned on me that what Elma was talking about was trows
– or trolls – and not in fact trowels. My cloth ears had never been
exposed much to the Shetland dialect and the conversation had
thrown me. Admittedly it doesn't take much to throw me. I'm
light as a feather up top.

Shetland has long been strong on superstitious beliefs. The
trows of Shetland are akin to the trolls of Norse mythology.
They're short, ugly, nocturnal creatures who live underground.
Just like Brochers. No, I retract that. Not like Brochers.

'And so then you took burning peat from the open fire and
you went round all the houses. They would boil a coo's head.
They would eat the meat and the old man of the house would

clean the head down to the bone and set it aside with a candle in the eye socket. In the morning, the head of the house would get up first and light the candle and go into the byre and he would give the cows a better feed that morning. And he would take a bottle of brandy – definitely smuggled – and go round every member of the household and give them a dram, from the very young to the very old. You just had to put your lips to it and he would say something like, "God be with you all these years", or some words like that. And there would be a better breakfast than normal.'

They certainly went to a lot of effort up here keeping those bloody trows at bay.

Elma told me about a young Shetland fiddle player who was obsessed with trows. 'He jist couldn't speak about nothing else. And he swears blind he seen one. I said, "Maurice, where did you see this thing?" He said, "I saw it on the hill. It was about three feet high."'

I looked out the car window and caught myself scanning the hills for trows.

I'd glanced out of a car window and got a shock once before. Clare was driving us to Aberdeen and we'd just passed Perth. I looked out of the passenger window and saw a panther in a field. It was staring at a neighbouring field of cows. I started waving my hands about, shouting 'What the f—?' and Clare instinctively looked in her rear-view mirror thinking I was yelling about some dangerous driver behind us. The driver behind us wasn't doing anything out of the ordinary but their front passenger was waving his hands about like I was and was probably shouting 'What the f—?' as well. He'd seen the panther too. 'It's a p-p-panther,' I stammered. 'There's a panther in the field.' It had been lying down and had suddenly got up. It was big, jet black and had pointy ears. It wasn't your ordinary cat: wrong thing, wrong environment. It should be in the jungle, not in a farmer's field on the outskirts of Perth. If it wasn't a panther, it was a jaguar. Either way it looked like Bagheera out of *The Jungle Book*. And it had no business being in a field on the edge of Perth. I was on edge and I know what I saw.

Then there was the time I looked out a train window near Stirling and saw a UFO in broad daylight. I'm not kidding. I wasn't the first to spot it either. The chap sitting across the table from me saw it first. We hadn't so much as said a word to each other since leaving Glasgow Queen Street until he pointed out the window and said, 'What's that?' He was pointing at a clear blue sky. Gliding gracefully across this clear blue sky was a small white lattice object. It looked like the Eiffel Tower, but I knew it wasn't the Eiffel Tower, because that's in Paris. It wasn't a smudge on the window either. We looked at each other and shrugged, almost lost for words. 'What is it?' said the man. 'I don't know,' I said. We were stumped. Our disbelieving eyes traced the curious structure as it cruised onwards and upwards and then, all of a sudden, it vanished into thin blue air. It was the strangest thing. We didn't really talk about it for the rest of the journey and went back to reading our papers. To this day I wonder what it was.

I'm not afraid to tell people – if the subject happens to crop up – that I saw a UFO. I'm not afraid to tell people – if the, um, subject crops up – that I saw a panther in a field in Perthshire. I'm not afraid to tell people that I saw the Loch Ness Monster, because I haven't seen the Loch Ness Monster. And I haven't seen any trows yet, though I kept my eyes on those hills.

I should have been up in Shetland investigating trows, not pretend Vikings. But Elma promised I wouldn't be disappointed with Up-Helly-Aa.

'It's a super festival. You'll never have seen anything like it in your life. It'll be brilliant tonight. There's no wind. If there's a lot of wind, the torches burn more quickly. But even when it's bad, it'll never be cancelled because of the weather. I mind going once when I was young and it took us two and a half hours to get there in the snow.'

We passed a Viking, standing in a lay-by. He had an axe on him too.

'It's so funny, the next morning,' laughed Elma. 'The people you meet in costume, they've never gone home and slept.'

The Vikings landed in Shetland over one thousand years ago and left their influence on the ways and customs of the islanders. For a long time, Shetland was under Nordic rule. It wasn't until 1469 that Shetland became part of Scotland. When Princess Margaret of Denmark married King James III of Scotland, both Shetland and Orkney were pledged by Margaret's father, King Christian I of Denmark, as security until a dowry was paid. It never was and Shetland and Orkney have remained with Scotland ever since. But Shetland does feel like another country, which it once was. They value their Nordic past and there's plenty nostalgia for the Vikings, even if they were mad bearded loons with bad manners.

I asked Elma if Up–Helly–Aa meant heavy drinking. I had this faint notion that it did.

'Everybody does drink too much,' admitted Elma, 'and what we really have trouble with these days is young folk drinking. But, as far as the quantity of alcohol being consumed goes, I dinna think there's really much change from the 1800s. The only thing is they would have had more of it for the period of time they had it. And then, when it was done, it was done.'

We entered Lerwick as a man on the pavement took a picture of the petrol station. Either he was a tourist or a petrol-station spotter. Both possibilities seemed bonkers to me.

Elma told me everything in Lerwick halted for Up–Helly–Aa. 'The Vikings have the power of the day. Everything stops.'

She dropped me off in the town centre. Elma had to get back

to her husband. Behind her natural ebullience there was heart-ache. Her husband was suffering from a brain tumour. Life wasn't easy or fair. 'It's very sad, very sad. It really is, for the whole family. We're all very sad to see such a capable, able man jist virtually reduced. He canna hardly talk. People visit the hoose and he'll struggle to converse with them and they'll say "He's not bad at all" but they dinna realise that when they're gone, he just goes.'

I said I hoped it hadn't been too much trouble picking me up at the airport and driving me here. I hadn't known about her difficult circumstances.

'I wanted to come,' said Elma. 'I felt I needed a bit of space myself. It's fine just to come out for a wee while, but he disna like to be left on his own. I think he's frightened of what's happening to him.'

I thanked Elma and wished her all the best. I'd have liked to spend more time with her. She was a great storyteller, but Up-Helly-Aa was of secondary importance. She had her day to get on with, her husband to care for. Elma gave me a wave and she drove off.

It was still pretty early. I'd normally be having my breakfast around about now but it felt more like lunchtime. I was standing in the middle of Lerwick at the Market Cross and could not fail to notice the giant board in front of me. A few tourists were studying it and taking photos. It was the Up-Helly-Aa Bill. This colourful proclamation had been put there by the Vikings first thing in the morning. It was anything but a sober announcement of Up-Helly-Aa and it took the mickey out of specially selected local targets, poking fun at the pompous and the useless in the eyes of the Vikings. It was, shall we say, irreverent and some of the words were harsh to say the least – these Vikings don't hold back. They're also partial to the odd dodgy joke and show a pronounced weakness for punning. This elaborately illustrated document revelled in local humour and gossip and much of it went over my head. But I had a go at deciphering it.

The Vikings, keen to cock a snook at the politicians, were questioning the wisdom of a new roundabout. Maybe one of their galleys had come a cropper on it. There was a jibe at a wind farm proposal and some carping at local councilors. Then there was the mention of 'hairy rejects from Kirkwall'. The 'hairy rejects' were the Kirkwall City Pipe Band, which Robert the Doonie was part of. Despite having Orkney on their passports, the pipers had been invited up to Shetland to blow their tunes for Up-Helly-Aa. I looked down the Bill as I tried to make more sense of some of it.

'Coming soon ON DA WATERFRONT: Big Bridder, the new Lerwick Reality TV show, needs flashers, winkers, byockers, muggers, buggers and piddlers: normal law-abiding citizens need not apply.'

Also the Vikings were demanding an explanation for a phenomenon that was vexing them.

'Why is Shetland Fudge harder and more sticky this time of year?'

One particularly venomous part of the Bill was a verse in the style of Little Jack Horner. It seemed to be a thinly veiled attack on an individual who had managed to attract the ire of the Vikings in the past year. Instead of 'what a good boy am I', the rhyme concluded: 'what a sanctimonious little shit-stirrer am I'.

The Bill ended with a chilling warning – in emphatic capital letters – for would-be vandals.

DEFACERS OF OUR BILL WILL HAVE THEIR BAGS SQUEEZED AND THEIR PIPES BLAWN BY A BIG HAIRY ORCADIAN!

BY ORDER AND UNDER THE SEAL OF THE GUISER JARL.

The seal of the Guiser Jarl involved a hand on an axe and next to it was the Vikings' motto:

WE AXE FOR WHAT WE WANT.

See what I mean about the puns? Mind you, if a punning Viking axed for my wallet, I would have to give him it. They had axes. I had a pen. And the axe is mightier than the pen.

I left the Bill behind and explored my surroundings. The shop windows were filled with Viking-related displays. There was a battle going on in one window between Up-Helly-Aa and Valentine's Day. Up-Helly-Aa had won. There were more helmets than chocolates.

The sign on the door of the chemist read 'Closed Wednesday for Up-Helly-Aa'. Tomorrow was a local holiday. You don't just go to work the morning after the biggest party this side of Valhalla.

I picked up a copy of the local paper. It was an Up-Helly-Aa special! I had a stab at the Viking crossword. One down: Viking god of thunder (4). That was an easy one. When I'd done with the crossword, I tackled the Up-Helly-Aa word search. Axe . . . galley . . . helmet . . .

I walked along the waterfront conscious of the fact I was walking in the footsteps of my dad. He must have gotten to know Lerwick like the back of his hand considering the number of times he'd ended up here waiting for a storm to blow over.

Then I saw the galley. Not that you could miss a Viking longship in broad daylight. It was going to be on display for most of the day while the Vikings went about their non-pillaging Up-Helly-Aa duties such as visiting schools and hospitals.

The 'hairy rejects' from Orkney were clambering all over the galley, the Kirkwall pipers posing for the photographers, lifting their pipes in the air. Despite the proliferation of big beards, I was still able to pick out Robert the Doonie and went over to say hello. I didn't mention The Ba' though I suppose Robert was over the disappointment by now and there was always next time. Robert told me that the band had already been in Lerwick three days, 'acclimatising ourselves'. He had a busy day ahead of him so

I let him get on with it and I checked out the galley myself. It was an impressive piece of craftsmanship and looked like any Viking longship I'd ever seen in a history book. It had taken months to build. And tonight those who built it would set it on fire. The dragon's head caught the low-lying sun and sparkled.

Overlooking the galley was Fort Charlotte with its silent canons pointing out into the bay. Seagulls squawked and swooped over the zigzagging parapet. A ferry chugged along beyond the galley. I fancied an early lunch. I'd been up since five. Within minutes my built-in radar had detected a chip shop and I decided to fortify myself with a white pudding supper. I wolfed it down in the knowledge that after a white pudding supper I wouldn't be able to eat anything for a very long time. The white pudding supper is surely the stodgiest option on the chip shop menu and I have a weakness for choosing it. You have to watch what you're doing though. You need to be extremely careful with a white pudding supper; you have to respect it. You must have something to wash it down with. My friend Andrew once made the near fatal error of buying a white pudding supper after a night out in Aberdeen and not buying a soft drink. He started to walk home scoffing his white pudding supper and before long he was choked up with white pudding and could barely breathe. It was touch and go for a while but he somehow made it back to his flat and gulped a gallon of water from the kitchen tap. Wiping the crumbs of white pudding from my face and draining my second can of Lilt (sometimes I like to keep it old-school), I rushed off so as not to be late for my afternoon appointment with Douglas.

Douglas is a historian and he knows a whole heap about Up-Helly-Aa. I'm sure there is not much Douglas doesn't know about Shetland. Lerwick-born, Douglas trained as a psychiatric nurse, later taught in Aberdeen, came back to Lerwick in the 1970s, and was in charge of the nursing school here. Technically in retirement now, Douglas conducts tours, like Elma. And like Elma, Douglas is a pleasure to listen to. I really enjoyed my couple of hours with him, walking the streets of Lerwick and learning all about Up-Helly-Aa.

Douglas set me straight right away by telling me that Up-Helly-Aa has more to do with the Victorians than the Vikings. Douglas dates Up-Helly-Aa from the 1880s. This epic festival may recall Shetland's Nordic ties, but the origin of the ceremony has little to do with the hairy marauders of a thousand years ago. Up-Helly-Aa is no Viking relic. Rather, it stems from some of the locals getting up to mischief.

Up-Helly-Aa arose from the need to put a stop to something: tar-barrelling. They used to behave like Brochers in Lerwick. In the mid-nineteenth century, a bunch of undesirables took to dragging burning barrels through Lerwick's narrow streets. It was a recipe for disaster. The Victorian middle classes didn't take too well to this tar-barrelling. The walls of their lovely houses bore the brunt of the smoke and filth.

Even before local revellers took to tar-barrelling, Lerwick was a raucous place during the festive season. A visiting Methodist missionary wrote of Lerwick in 1824 that 'the whole town was in uproar' and described a restless 24-hour period with the 'blowing of horns, beating of drums, tinkling of old tin kettles, firing of guns, shouting, bawling, fiddling, fifeing, drinking and fighting'. I hoped not to encounter any fifeing this night.

There was pressure on town officials to act on the tar-barrelling and, in 1874, they banned it. But they had to replace it with something. They sought a more controlled affair and decided a torchlight procession would be fitting. Later on came the Vikings and the galley.

The festival became known as Up-Helly-Aa, the literal meaning of which isn't totally clear. There is some evidence that in rural parts of Shetland they once celebrated Uphalliday (end of the holidays, or end of the holy days) 24 days after Christmas, harking back to the Pagan festival of Yule. 'But in any case,' said Douglas, 'Up-Helly-Aa is linked with notions of bonfires and welcoming the sun after a long winter. It was very much about feasting and merrymaking.'

The first galley was built in 1889 and then the Bill appeared. 'Initially it just gave instructions to the guisers. And then it got a wee bit more elaborate.' Lerwick has long had a tradition of guising, of putting on costume during the festive season. In Up-Helly-Aa only the main squad – the Guiser Jarl's squad – dress up as Vikings. The other squads pick their own themes. A lot of the men seem to end up dressed as women. Hence Up-Helly-Aa's alternative name: Transvestite Tuesday.

'By 1903 the guising was getting a bit big for private houses,' explained Douglas, ever the historian with his dates, 'so they opened a couple of halls to which the guisers were invited.' These are the invite-only hall parties that go on all night and are an integral part of Up-Helly-Aa. A dozen halls are open all over Lerwick and I had secured a ticket for the party at Bells Brae Primary School. The burning of the galley is what sticks in most people's minds about Up-Helly-Aa, but the evening's focus shifts to feasting and revelry. Each squad must visit the halls in rotation and perform their sketch for the guests. The sketch might involve local parody, topical satire or total nonsense.

'Some you'll get. Some you won't. Some nobody gets,' said Douglas, shaking his head. 'You think "What the hell are they meant to be doing?" They're varied. One year a woman next to me said, "Well, that last squad was bad but that one jist noo jist took the biscuit." You might get Amy Winehoose or Gordon Brown, something topical, or local things. Some are really good. The secret is you don't tell anyone what you'll be doing. Some guisers don't even tell their wives.'

Douglas went on: 'As a guest at the hall, you get a free feed.'

He then informed me that 'they are renowned in Bells Brae for their reestit mutton soup.' I looked forward to trying it. 'There's no drinking in the hall itself, but there is a designated area. There are a thousand drunk guys going around the halls but there's really no trouble. There'll be internal squabbles and they're kept pretty much in check, because if you are in the squad and you go to a hall, you are responsible for your behaviour. If you are squad leader and there is a serious fight, the squad will be banned for a year. So there is an incentive not to misbehave.

'A lot of the older guys will be having a sleep just now because it's a long night. You have to watch. You'll find twilight bits where you won't know where you are. You have an obligation to go for a dance, though the guisers have priority. And that's how it sort of works. God knows how many have met girlfriends. Though I'm no' saying it's a dating agency!'

Douglas wasn't going to a hall party tonight. 'I was asked one year and I went along. I hated it. Really did. Most boring night I'd had in me life. All I could see was the squads of boys coming. I wished I was away with them.'

He'd had the honour of being a Viking in the Guiser Jarl's squad a couple of years ago. Douglas talked about a visitor from Germany who had also been asked to join the Guiser Jarl's squad. 'He was from Berlin and he had come here on holiday years ago and got bitten by a Shetland pony. He was so fascinated he came for Up-Helly-Aa every year and, to his great delight, he was invited. And he loved it.

'The Guiser Jarl can invite anybody he wants. So if you had been friendly with him at university or something, there's a chance you would be in the Jarl squad. With the other squads, well, the oil came and the population grew and there was a danger of the thing becoming too big. So a ruling was made: you had to have been a resident of Lerwick for at least five years to get onto a squad. Recently they changed the criteria and you need to have been resident in Shetland for five years.'

Douglas explained the process of how someone gets to be Guiser Jarl, the figurehead of Up-Helly-Aa. Jarl is the Old Norse for earl. 'First, you need to be elected onto the Up-Helly-Aa committee. There is a big meeting of guisers and names are put forward. If you've had a big interest in Up-Helly-Aa and you've gone and made torches in the galley shed . . . It's not a closed shop, but you need to be particularly interested. Once you're on the committee you know that in fifteen years' time you will be Guiser Jarl. So it's a pretty long apprenticeship. But since you know your time will come, you make preparations for it. There's a lot of money to be raised. You need to go round all the businesses collecting, and they would be expected to contribute. The money goes towards things like the wood for the galley and the torches.'

We walked through the cobbled lanes of Old Lerwick. There were fishing nets by people's front gates. 'They're herring nets,' explained Douglas. 'They're given out free by the council. Monday morning, when you put your black bags out, you cover them up to keep them from the seagulls.'

Douglas summed up what he believed Up-Helly-Aa to be about. 'It's really a festival and you can ask "what's behind all this?" and "what are the benefits?" Well, in my opinion, after the long winter it really is – from a mental health point of view – something to look forward to. It's a community thing and I don't think you can really feel it unless you were born in Lerwick. It'll be the same with Burghead and their Clavie. Some folk will think it's great. Others will think it's a lot of rubbish, burning things.

'There's mythology and culture attached to it, but people really enjoy it. Here's a chance to put on your party clothes, meet your friends, stay oot all night if you want. Stay for an hour if you want. But you're seeing people, meeting people. After a bleak winter, it's jist an excuse to go oot for a dram. "Let's make something o this." It's very much aboot community spirit. Everybody here looks forward to Up-Helly-Aa.'

It can confuse the Norwegian tourists. 'On the tours I get Norwegians scratching their heads. I don't think they're too keen on the Viking link being a big thing here. It's not one of the most heroic pasts.' Then there are those who take exception to the fact that there are no women in the procession. 'You do get an element saying it's sexist. I had a rough ride with one group of tourists.' Douglas remembered the year there was a one-man demonstration against Up-Helly-Aa, for religious reasons. 'This religious guy had a placard calling for a ban and nobody was giving a hoot for him. They were jist ignoring him. Anyone that religious-minded shouldn't go to Up-Helly-Aa. People can go to the kirk or whatever they want to do. And people that want to can go to Up-Helly-Aa. If you find a festival and it works, you keep it. Maybe you change things and freshen it up. That keeps things going. It'll go for a few years yet.'

As someone who had just dropped in for the day, I wondered what the locals thought of the tourists descending on Lerwick for Up-Helly-Aa. 'It used to be a bone of contention but it really has resolved itself. Folk were saying: "It's not for tourists; it's for locals." Well, of course it's for locals. It's for everybody. You want people to enjoy themselves and return.'

Lerwick isn't the only Up-Helly-Aa in Shetland. Certainly it's the biggest and the most spectacular, but there are several others, on smaller scales. The likes of Northmavine, Brae and Uyea-sound on Unst all have their midwinter celebrations. Some of them even set their boats on the water. In Lerwick, the galley doesn't touch the sea. The burning site is a playing field. Rural Shetlanders mock the Lerwegians for burning their boat in a play park. The people of Lerwick regard Shetland's other fire festivals as not being up to scratch. And they make sure they call them fire festivals.

'It's a wee bit tongue-in-cheek,' said Douglas. 'Lerwick is Up-Helly-Aa and the rest are fire festivals. The country ones take it almost as serious, but not quite. They let women in and it's a small self-contained thing – and it works.'

It was time for Douglas to leave me. We were near Shetland Museum. Douglas had let me know that the Jarl and his squad were expected to be at the museum as part of their day's programme. It was an opportunity to catch the Vikings at close quarters ahead of the evening procession. I thanked Douglas for his time and we parted.

Walking into the museum was like wandering onto the set of *The Lord of the Rings*. The Jarl's squad looked like they'd be marching off to Minas Tirith in a minute. Maybe they had a showdown with Saruman and his Orcs (the Orcs, in this case, being the Orcadians).

The Jarl and his squad had taken over the Shetland Museum. It was a fine opportunity for tourists – or anyone really – to mingle and perhaps have their picture taken with a Norseman. One Viking was left holding the baby. I hoped he wasn't stealing it. The sun was setting now as the Kirkwall Pipe Band played at the waterside. The Vikings were letting the public try on their helmets. Needless to say, they were heavy. Until today, the Vikings' outfits had been strictly under wraps, the theme a closely guarded secret. Now they were revealed in all their glory. Their chest medallions carried the legend Kol Kalison. Each year, the Guiser Jarl picks his theme, electing some prominent Norse figure. Kol Kalison, who lived in the twelfth century, supervised the construction of St Magnus Cathedral in Kirkwall. This year's Guiser Jarl, Roy Leask, was a construction company director and many members of his squad worked in the local construction industry. So the selection of Kol Kalison seemed fitting.

Making the Vikings' outfits wasn't cheap. It cost a whopping £1,600 to kit out each warrior and plenty thought and effort had gone into the design and execution. It really was intricate work. All told, the ornate costumes took months to make. These Vikings wanted to look their best. The firm that supplied the gold-plated chainmail had worked on *Gladiator*. The Jarl's squad wore brown leather boots and dark green leggings. These Vikings had their knees covered up. The outfits weighed up to 43lbs; it was heavy work. The Jarl stood out from his squad in his silver chainmail and winged helmet. The helmets of the squad members detailed the galley.

The Vikings formed a large circle in the museum foyer. A horn was blown. It sounded like a cross between a wolf and a cow. The Jarl stood in the middle of the circle. Not only was he the first Jarl to grace this magnificent modern museum, he'd helped build it. He was the main contractor for the job. Roy had learned his trade as a joiner next door to where the museum stood now. 'I think I can class myself as being the last of the Dock Boys,' said Roy to loud cheers. The Dock Boys were Lerwick's strong tradition of skilled carpenters. They'd built the first galleys a hundred years ago. It made a change from building boats and battleships. Roy had been building galleys for almost 40 years. This year's galley was called *Breckon*. It was named after both his dog and his favourite beach in North Yell.

'Seeing as Roy is here, I'd like him to fix the window for us!' suggested the curator of the museum to much laughter. The Jarl presented him with a shield for the museum's collection. There were hip-hip-hoorays and the Jarl declared that any visitors to Shetland were more than welcome and that he hoped they would enjoy the evening. There was a generous spirit in an impressive space the stout Vikings filled well. There were more than 70 men and boys in the Jarl's squad, including Roy's son and grandson. The extent of the family affair even stretched to the pipe band, which was led by Roy's daughter who'd piped her dad into the Town Hall in the morning. There can't have been a prouder man in Lerwick on the last Tuesday of January than Roy Leask.

The Vikings then launched into 'The Galley Song', an Up-Helly-Aa tradition. 'Every guiser has a duty', they belted out before it all went a bit Disney and they segued into zip-a-dee-do-dah. Between that and the shiny costumes and the museum surroundings it would be tempting to say that it all felt quite touristy and schmaltzy, but at the same time you couldn't take your eyes off them. To all intents and purposes, they looked like Vikings. They had axes! And helmets! And beards! 'Mr Blue-bird's on my shoulder . . .' Okay, so it was faintly ridiculous.

Once they'd stopped singing I got chatting to a couple of Vikings. And I'm afraid to say, I couldn't resist having my picture taken with them. It wasn't every day you met a Viking and here I was meeting two. The tourist in me leapt out. They were nice Vikings, not horrible at all. I told them I had been lucky enough to get a ticket for one of the hall parties later on and that I looked forward to witnessing their dramatic arrival. 'He's a whisky, I'm a brandy,' said one of the Vikings. Maybe I'd see them at the bar then.

Their boss man, the Guiser Jarl, had a few final words for the crowd. 'For those here for their first Up-Helly-Aa . . . it's a beautiful night and I'm sure you'll not be disappointed!'

The Jarl and his men had been granted the freedom of Lerwick for 24 hours and the Jarl had promised to leave the town the way he found it, which was nice of him. They'd had a long and exhausting day of engagements but the main act was yet to come, and then the all-night partying after that. It was hard work being a Viking. Their bus was waiting for them. The Vikings hopped aboard, a couple of them stamping out their fags first. 'See ye later Jeemy,' cried a Viking, waving his axe.

With the Vikings gone and the museum about to close its doors, I walked back towards the town centre, passing a butcher advertising 'freshly shot haggis' and Posers, 'the number one nightclub in Scotland'. Ah, but is it really better than Joanna's in Elgin?

I nipped into a pub. I just made last orders. It was half past five but this was no ordinary night. Two Vikings stood at the bar. A man walked in. He was wearing pyjamas and a dressing gown. 'Sorry, we're closed,' said the barman. The man shrugged and went out the door. I guessed he was going to be part of the procession and wasn't sleepwalking at tea-time. After my pint, I saw another strange sight on the street. (I'd see a thousand strange sights by the end of the night.) Two policemen were talking to a man in a top hat. The man in the top hat looked like he was about to topple over. He was unsteady on his feet and uncertain in his speech. Eventually the police let him go and he walked into a wall.

There was a last-minute run on the off-licence. Half of Lerwick was getting their orders in for the all-nighter ahead. Up-Helly-Aa demands a monster-size carry out. Luckily, the off-licence had anticipated demand and had enough supplies to cope. Crates of beer were piled high. Cider was proving popular. Lemonade and coke were bought for mixers and a six-foot chicken plucked four cans of Special Brew off the shelf. The chicken then decided he needed a bottle of rum as well. I bought a few bottles of beer and stashed them in my backpack. I couldn't turn up at the hall party empty-handed. I knew there was a bar area but I figured it was a bring-your-own affair.

Up-Helly-Aa felt a lot closer now. A pair of hillbillies in straw hats chatted to Dracula outside the British Legion. Traffic was becoming noticeably heavier with the procession not far away and spectators looking to find parking spaces. I made for the Town Hall, with its huge stained-glass windows. The Vikings were inside for their dinner. After they'd been fed, their procession would start just along the road. Across from the Town Hall was the war memorial. Douglas had recommended it as an excellent place to watch the procession and the galley burning from. True enough you could see the burning site down the hill. A few Up-Helly-Aa enthusiasts were in position already, making certain they'd have a good view of the proceedings.

The Raven Banner – red flag, black raven – fluttered above the Town Hall. In Norse mythology, a pair of ravens sat on Odin's shoulders and told him everything that went on in the world.

A distracted Viking walked past, engrossed in the text message he was sending. It probably said RAID.

A Norwegian television crew was hovering about. The male presenter grabbed hold of a Viking to interview him. I eavesdropped.

Interview with a Viking:

[Presenter] How long have you been in the . . . ah . . . tradition?

[Viking] Since I was a boy.

[Presenter] I have to ask you about the moustache.

[Viking] Beard. We grow them specially.

[Presenter] What do you think of Wikings?

[Viking] They were warriors, real people.

[Presenter] I don't think the women were in charge.

Silence . . .

The presenter was having a hard time of it. Vikings don't interview well. At least this one didn't. The hapless interviewer went for Plan B. He produced a plastic helmet and put it on. The Viking wasn't impressed.

[Viking] That's a fake one.

The presenter became desperate.

[Presenter] RrrrraaaaAAARRRGGGHHHH!

It was less the roar of a Viking than the roar of a despairing Norwegian television presenter. Perhaps unwisely, the Norwegian television presenter also waved his hands in his subject's face.

[Presenter] Was I scary?

[Viking] No.

At least the presenter had more joy on the subject of King Christian of Denmark. The Viking knew his history.

[Viking] He pawned Shetland and didn't buy it back again.

[Presenter] Ah-ha! Shetland would have been Norwegian.

[Viking] And then we would have had the whole of the North Sea oil between us.

Pause . . .

[Viking] I have to go in for the evening meal now.

And with that the Viking marched back into the Town Hall.

Another Viking, who'd taken his chainmail off, popped out for a fag and a breather. As long as the Norwegian TV presenter didn't get a hold of him.

The pipe band and the brass band were warming up. The mad top hatter I'd seen earlier being questioned by the police was swaying about in the street. 'I hear the horns! I hear the horns!' he shouted. He started marching (in a fashion) behind the pipe band, arms flailing. He did a little shimmy, played a lot of air guitar and then tried some air bagpipes. The crowd was amused. The man was deranged.

Hundreds of people had lined up on top of a grass verge that acted as a natural grandstand for the procession. The anticipation was building and the temperature was plummeting. The squads were beginning to assemble, waiting to collect their torches. With those torches, they would destroy four months of hard work and the galley would be no more. I examined the costumes of some of the squads. They were a ragtag lot, truth be told. There were nurses, ducks, Cavaliers, Egyptians, leprechauns,

Goldilockses, monks, angels, devils and road sweepers. What a motley crew. Up-Helly-Aa definitely wasn't all about Vikings.

The Jarl and his sated squad emerged from the Town Hall, making blood-curdling roars and brandishing their axes in the air. They marched up the ranks of men. There was a call and response and then the streetlights were switched off. A hush descended on the crowd. This was it. You could cut the atmosphere with an axe.

The Jarl stood proudly on the stern of his galley with his axe raised. The dragon's teeth were shining. Vikings flanked the galley with standard bearers at the front. I smelled paraffin in the cold night air. 'Alright lads, everybody got a torch?' At half past seven the silence was severed, the darkness broken by a maroon splitting the sky with its loud whoosh. All the tension was pierced by the bang. Suddenly we were treated to the intense orange of the lit torches. The Jarl appeared, through the thick smoke, in dramatic silhouette. People cheered and took pictures. The torches were like giant matchsticks. You could hear them burn. The temperature must have jumped ten degrees, or so it seemed. When all of the thousand or so torches were burning and the entire route was illuminated, it took the breath away. It was quite simply one of the most incredible things I've seen in my life: a mesmerising trail of fire, as far as the eye could see. I'll never forget that never-ending line of hypnotic flames.

The galley moved forward between the ranks of torches. The bands played and the squads of guisers counter-marched. Down the brae they went, singing the 'Up-Helly-Aa Song'. 'Roll their glory down the ages, sons of warriors and sages.' Women spectators picked out their men from the squads. There was lots of laughing and joking. The Jarl waved from his galley and no one failed to wave back. This was sheer pageantry, but it was spectacular.

Down St Olaf Street, along King Harald Street and then enter the dragon to the burning site. The torch bearers were still singing as they entered the walled arena. Soon all of them, a thousand guisers, had surrounded the doomed galley. The Jarl called out for praise. 'Three cheers for the men who built the torches!' Hurray. 'Three cheers for the men who built the galley!' Hurray. 'Three cheers for Up-Helly-Aa!' Hurray. And then it was 'Three cheers for the Guiser Jarl!' The Jarl jumped out of his galley before another maroon struck the sky. 'The Galley Song' was sung and then there was the sound of a bugle. After the last note the guisers started throwing their torches into the galley. Within seconds, it was engulfed in flames. For a brief moment I saw the stars, before the smoke cloaked them. There was the traditional rendering of 'The Norseman's Home' in the face of the inferno. 'Then let us all in harmony, give honour to the brave, the noble, hardy, northern men, who ruled the stormy wave.' The mast and sail were being eaten by the flames. I could still make out the dragon's head. I was some distance from the galley on the other side of the wall but I could feel the warmth of the boat bonfire. Sparks of cinder floated down on us and I worried my coat was going to catch fire. In all honesty, I struggled to get a proper view of the burning of the galley because I was standing behind two Dutch giants. Both were filming with their video cameras, and one of the giants was using his free hand to direct. It was very annoying. They were obscuring my view, but I wasn't about to tap a giant on the shoulder and say, 'Excuse me, I can't see.' I adjusted my position and managed to get a slightly better view. Space was at a premium. But little wonder so many people wanted to watch this.

When it was over, spent torches lay strewn around the remains of the blackened galley, evidence of arson. Vikings took pictures of each other with the destruction as the backdrop. The crowd began to disperse, bottles clinking in carry-out bags. There were destinations and intentions. At least I had a party to go to. A bunch of monks stood slugging cider on a street corner. A leprechaun jumped on a bus full of leprechauns. This night would get stranger still.

I got to Bells Brae and showed my ticket to the men at the door. I then had to find Annalene and thank her. It was she who had got me the ticket after my initial enquiry to Elma. Annalene was busy in the kitchen making soup and sandwiches. At Up-Helly-Aa, the men perform and the women feed them. It's the way it is. I thanked Annalene for my passport to the evening and handed her the money for the ticket. She said she hoped I'd enjoy myself. The band was playing from the stage and there was already dancing on the floor. I found a seat in the corner and waited for the first squad to arrive. Each squad had to perform their sketch at all the halls in the long night ahead. When they'd finished their sketch, they had a dance – of their choice – with the ladies of the hall. The squad then moved on to the next hall . . . and repeat until daybreak. Straightaway it was heartening to see all the generations together – grannies, wives, children – having a good time.

The sketch element was a whirlwind of daftness. One of the sketches involved three ducks. One of the ducks collapsed and the other two got the vet who declared the duck dead but the other ducks wanted a second opinion. The vet brought in a dog. The dog sniffed the duck and the vet said the duck was definitely dead. The other ducks demanded a third opinion so the vet introduced a cat. The cat sniffed the duck and the vet confirmed that the duck was most certainly dead. The vet's bill came to £500 and the ducks queried it. The vet explained that the initial consultation was £20 but because of the LAB report and the CAT scan it was £500. This is the sort of thing you can expect at Up-Helly-Aa.

Squad Number 45 arrived. The SWRI: Shetland Women

Running Idle. Grown men dressed up as old ladies, and gross caricatures of old ladies at that. I'm not sure what some of the real old ladies in the hall thought of it. The squad of old ladies sat down on chairs in the middle of the room. The hypnotist – for there was a hypnotist, not a real one mind you – began with his act. 'Good evening, girls. Can I just say how gorgeous you're all looking. Boy, am I going to have some fun with you tonight. You'll be doing things you've never dreamed of. Now look into my eyes and . . . sleep.' The old ladies slumped in their seats. The hypnotist continued. 'When I say "knickers" you will misbehave appropriately.' Soon enough the old ladies were performing a striptease, throwing off their headscarves and the rest. It was horrific. The wrinkly face masks made them look like Zelda out of 'The Terrahawks'. And now the Zeldas were nearly naked.

I needed a drink. I went looking for the bar and found it in the school staffroom. There was quite a crowd. I got talking to three fishermen from Fraserburgh. Their boat had broken down and they were stuck in Lerwick. I smiled to myself as I thought about my dad. They couldn't have picked a better night to be stuck in Lerwick and were in possession of a sizable carry-out.

After a while I got my confidence back and felt brave enough to catch some more sketches. It was a tight squeeze in the school corridor with all the false bellies and musical instruments. I almost tripped over a camel. 'Is that camel alright?' I asked its Moroccan owner. 'Aye, he's jist tired,' replied the man. I knew he was Moroccan because he was wearing a T-shirt that said 'Moroccans on tour Up-Helly-Aa 2008' on the back with the names of all the halls – instead of Paris, Hamburg, Copenhagen, etc. The camel looked out for the count. I think it'd been on the hookah.

When I returned to the hall it was worse than the striptease grannies. Moulin Huge were doing the can-can with their stomachs hanging out. Their feathers were flying and their fishnet stockings were stretched. It was less Lady Marmalade and more Man Marmalade. I rubbed my eyes but the filthy French dancers were still there. The next act featured a man pulling a brolly from his arse.

My head was spinning and I'd only had the one beer so far. It was like Dylan and the Magic Roundabout – backwards. I popped out for some fresh air. One of the Moulin Huge ladies was smoking a cigarette by the door. A man hurried into the building and she shouted, 'Aye, ye're late, ye missed it,' and gave him a flash of her false boobs. Mademoiselle Moulin Huge then invited me on the back of her lorry. I think she was joking. Then she got serious. 'It's a bit of a step doon this, being in the Jarl's squad last year, being a warrior, and now this, being made up to look like a lady-of-sorts.' I told her she looked very nice. We were interrupted by a striptease granny who showed me her handbag and its benefits. 'It's handy. You can store drink in it.' She/he laughed. 'Aye, you'll get away with it one day a year here.' I said she should be allowed to carry an alcohol-concealing handbag at any time of year. Meanwhile an accordionist climbed on the back of a truck. He was off to his next gig with his squad. 'Aye, it's an affa cerry on, Up-Helly-Aa,' he cried to me. 'It's fucking awesome.'

The beauty of having a monumental booze-up at the end of January.

I bumped into another Gary in the school corridor. He didn't know who he was supposed to be. His only clue was that he was wearing a suit. I couldn't help him. A boy and girl stumbled out of a walk-in cupboard. They must have been looking for a mop. Or maybe they just wanted a quiet moment to themselves. It's not easy finding peace during Up-Helly-Aa. 'Some guys get drunk . . . some guys get lucky,' said the other Gary, taking another gulp of his beer. A group of GIs in the corridor were wondering when they should be leaving for the next hall so that they remained on schedule. 'Ten minutes?' Up-Helly-Aa is mostly about having fun but it's about sticking with the plan, too. You can't be getting too comfortable. There are always more people to entertain with your truck awaiting you to transport you to the next venue. Just then Top Cat came running out of the hall chased by Officer Dibble. I went back to the bar, where I met a Transformer, or a robot in disguise. He told me how he and his fellow Transformers had turned their truck into a galley. I was sorry I'd missed that. 'You wouldn't do it again, would you?' I asked him. The Transformer shook his head.

I caught up with Annalene and her husband. He reckoned you couldn't have a night like this anywhere else. 'It never gets out of hand. There's rarely trouble. Everyone is enjoying themselves too much to cause any bother.' Douglas had said the same. This night was over-the-top but it was never out-of-order. People were high-spirited, not mean-spirited.

It was all happening in the hall though. The Jarl and his squad had arrived. For the hall guests, this was the highlight of the evening, the moment they'd most looked forward to. All the Vikings had to do was stand there and dazzle in their chainmail and the crowd applauded. The Vikings delved into their repertoire of Up-Helly-Aa songs and the women were invited by the Norsemen to dance. None of the Vikings was turned down. There was no sketch from the Jarl's squad. They didn't need one. They just had to show up and the night was theirs. 'Three cheers for the Jarl and his squad!' 'Three cheers for the host and hostess!' And with that, they were gone.

A basketball player high-fived me and I was pecked at by a pink flamingo. Time to venture outside again, where more nutty scenes awaited me. An angel fell out of a lorry and landed on his wings. It looked sore. The angel lay on the road laughing, as if it was the funniest thing ever. He got up and straightened his crumpled wings, just as a SWAT team descended on the scene. Surely to God they weren't taking out the angel.

I took in the SWAT team's sketch. It seemed to consist of them running round the hall swatting flies and shouting 'die flea, die'.

There was no 'what time is it?' at Up–Helly–Aa. Time had flown out the window.

A fly walked into the bar. This isn't the beginning of a bad joke. A fly walked into the bar and cracked open a can of beer. Even holding the can, he still had five hands free. It must be fun being a bar fly. Now that was a bad joke. A gorilla and a sheep were getting to know each other in the corner. An angel was having a minor disagreement with the Devil. I got talking to a human being. She was Aileen from Glasgow. Aileen had lived in Lerwick for the past three years. I told her I was here for a festival book and she recommended I put the Big Bannock in my diary. I made a mental note to do just that. Then I forgot. Aileen said the women thought the men weren't dancing enough. Too many guisers were making a beeline for the bar, leaving the women without dancing partners. I admitted I wasn't much help. I said that if I had my kilt on I might have taken part in the ceilidh dancing. This didn't wash with Aileen. She told me that was a poor excuse. And it was. I was just another selfish bloke in the bar.

Aileen was of the opinion that Up–Helly–Aa was mainly an excuse for a good piss-up. 'But when you say that,' she said, 'some people get annoyed. They defend it and say it's tradition.' That made it a traditional piss-up then? I mentioned how mad the sketches were. Aileen said the sketches flew over the heads of a lot of Lerwegians too. But she liked living up here in Shetland. In the summer she wouldn't wish to be anywhere else.

I was feeling hungry. Between the dance-floor and the kitchen was a makeshift cafe where you could sit yourself down and scoff sandwiches and cakes and slurp cups of tea to your heart's content. I sat down and scoffed sandwiches and cakes and

Left.
A Warm Welcome to Kirkwall. Sorry, we can't help you; The Ba's on today.

Below.
All Rise. Hands up if you're an Uppie . . . or a Doonie.

Up-Helly-Alley Cats. Top Cat and the gang smoke out Officer Dibble.

So Long, Longship. What happens when you give a bunch of Vikings a box of matches.

Vintage Vagrant. A hooched-up Robert Fergusson offers the author a slug of port.

St Andrews Supergroup: Bishop Kennedy, Kate Kennedy, The Marshall of the Procession and The Keeper of the Costumes.

Hold Your Horses. The beauty of Langholm Common Riding.

Auld Style. There's something fishy about the Barley Bannock crew (especially the one on the far left).

Above.
How to Water a Plant. The Burry Man wets his whistle with whisky.

Left.
Off His Trolley. It dawns on the Burry Man that he doesn't have a pound coin.

Blow Hard. Two men in a shed are unmoved by the passion of a piper at the Birnam Highland Games.

A Truly Offal Sight. Hungry hopefuls tuck in at the World Haggis Eating Championships.

Above.
Neigh Bother. The
Festival of the Horse at
St Margaret's Hope on
South Ronaldsay.

Left.
Plough On.
Concentration is key
and advice is given at the
Boys' Ploughing Match
on the Sands o'Wright.

The Spectacle of The Clavie. There's no smoke without Brochers.

The Fury of the Fireballs. Some spectacular swinging in Stonehaven.

slurped cups of tea. The mountain of sandwiches was replenished every five minutes. It was all the sandwiches in the world. I spotted a sheep spooning some of Bells Brae's famous reestit mutton soup. That couldn't be right. I couldn't resist trying some of the reestit mutton soup for myself. It was marvellous. I had another bowl. I then asked for a glass of water and was offered more soup. I was all souped up. Who eats soup at four in the morning anyway?

I crossed paths again with Robert the Doonie. Bells Brae was his seventh hall of the night. Robert revealed he was a piper down. 'He fell and split his head.' Robert was still stunned by the procession and being part of it. 'It was amazing going through the torches with the pipes.'

I sat down in the hall and then disaster struck. I was invited to join in the Eightsome Reel. If anything was going to mark me out as a foolish visitor, it was my inability to accomplish the Eightsome Reel. Up here they are born dancing the Eightsome Reel. The last time I'd attempted it – at a friend's wedding – I'd got the helicopters. Mid-spin I had to stop. I was reeling. With one hand on my forehead and the other held out as if to say 'stop, please, stop' I rocked back and forth on the spot. I knew everyone was laughing at me but I was past caring. I just wanted the helicopter ride to stop. 'Black Hawk down,' cried my friend Brian, doubled up with laughter as he wiped tears of mirth from his eyes.

Thankfully I didn't provide a repeat performance at Bells Brae but it was still a wretched display from yours clueless. I single-handedly and wrong-footedly turned the Eightsome Reel into a drunken tarantula. I think I may have confused it with the Canadian Barn Dance or something. Whatever I'd done, I'd let the side down. Though it was their fault for asking me. I sought sanctuary in the bar where I could keep my two left feet under the table.

It was the twilight hour Douglas had warned me about. Everything felt other. The hall was thinning out. The sketches were even less polished. The three cheers from the squad leaders sounded more slurred. I decided I may as well head for the bus station. I had to catch the first bus anyway in order to make my flight. I'd checked that the bus service to the airport was actually operating the morning after Up-Helly-Aa. It was. As long as the bus driver hadn't been overdoing it in one of the squads.

My last – and lasting – image from Bells Brae was a gorilla circling the hall on a bicycle.

I staggered through the streets of Lerwick in the pre-dawn. A truck full of rednecks sped by with The Beatles blaring. 'Help me if you can.' A lorry-load of sheep zoomed past. 'Oggy oggy oggy.' The mobile discos continued their early-morning deliveries of squads to their next hall appointments. Parties raged in the backs of those trucks. One squad tried to tempt a group of girls on board for some Up-Helly-Aa hospitality but the invitation was flat-out rejected. 'Why can't you just dress as Vikings?' complained the girls to the cowboys. They wanted real warriors, not cattle-hands.

Daybreak in Lerwick. Had the night really happened or had I dreamt it? I made check-in by four minutes and was back in Glasgow by breakfast time. I'd been slapped in the face by Up-Helly-Aa but nothing would wake me up once my head hit that pillow.

Whuppity Whit?

Clare and I caught the train from Glasgow to Lanark. The driving rain meant we could barely see out of the window. The weather was terrible. The weather was Scotland. But hey, it was a day out. A temporary escape from the city in the foulest conditions imaginable. 'So what's Whumpity Scoonie?' my wife asked as the carriage rattled and pellets struck the glass inches from our faces.

'Whuppity Scoorie,' I corrected her, 'is an old Scottish custom.'

'Is it any good?'

'Any good? Of course it's good. It's an old Scottish custom.'

'I see.'

Clare wasn't exactly embracing the spirit of Whuppity Scoorie. I detected a degree of scepticism in her voice. Wait till she got to Lanark, I thought. Then she'd see what Whuppity Scoorie was all about. 'We're nearly there,' I said, trying to sound upbeat, but failing miserably, as the rat-tat-tat of the rain kept up.

If you've never heard of Whuppity Scoorie, then you've never lived. In Lanark. Every year, on the first of March, the local children run three times round the church and chase the Devil out of town. Just like children do in every other town up and down the country, or maybe not.

The market town of Lanark is one of Scotland's oldest Royal Burghs. The place positively reeks of tradition. It honks of history. It takes a place like Lanark to dream up something like Whuppity Scoorie and run with it.

I said something back there about children chasing the Devil but there are multiple theories about the true meaning of Whuppity Scoorie.

Here's one of them. The children, by sprinting round the church, are celebrating the arrival of spring, something to get excited about after the long winter. Even if today was clearly still winter.

The children carry weapons. Paper weapons. Not paper guns, but paper balls on string. And they swing these paper balls above their heads, landing repeat blows on Beelzebub, if you happen to side with the Devil theory. Scapegoating Satan is a national pastime in Scotland. We've been quick to blame Ol' Red Eyes for a lot of things that have gone wrong in our country (when it's not him, it's the English). It's the Devil's fault the trains never run on time. It's the Devil's fault it's forever raining. And it's the Devil's fault Scotland have never won the World Cup. In fact, he's been particularly diabolical in recent years by not letting us anywhere near the World Cup finals. Auld Nick is an arsehole.

Still on the theme of evil, a 'whuppity scoorie' might have been a nimble sprite with a malicious bent. Such bad fairies threatened the crops and animals during the winter. It was high time these spiteful pixies were gotten rid of, before they ruined the harvest. How? By sprinting round the church three times, that's how. Anticlockwise too, or else it doesn't work.

Another wispy theory links Whuppity Scoorie with religious penance and particularly the (now discontinued) practice of whipping scoundrels thrice round the church (anticlockwise) before cleansing (or scooring) the scoundrels in the River Clyde. I would have hated to be a scoundrel in those days.

One thing I like about Scottish festivals is that people insist on keeping them going but have no idea why these festivals came about in the first place. Or at least they're not sure. The Clavie falls into this murky category. I'm all for it.

Clare and I stepped off the train into the rain and were swept away to Lanark Cross, the customary setting for Whuppity Scoorie. St Nicholas Church was under renovation and was shrouded in scaffolding, surrounded by a perimeter security fence.

There were lots of watchful parents and excited children milling around. The children were already jumping about with their paper balls on string. They were clearly into Whuppity Scoorie in a big way. It was good to see. That we were presently in the midst of the perfect storm didn't deter them in the slightest, which was as it should be – as long as the scaffolding didn't fall on top of them.

The Whuppity Scoorie MC stepped onto the podium in front of the scaffolding and got on the mike to address a crowd who were mad enough for Whuppity Scoorie to be out on a night such as this.

'Testing . . . testing . . .'

The wind was howling and the rain was bucketing down. Oh for a bit of sun.

'Thank you for coming out on such a miserable night. It's a very abbreviated version of Whuppity Scoorie tonight. But your participation will ensure these rituals of ours will survive for a long, long time. Welcome to our quirky little ways.'

Nicely put, I thought. The children were on tenterhooks. They were chomping at the bit. They just wanted to get started and batter the Devil.

'Will all the big ones make their way to the front please, and all the wee ones go to the back.'

The boys and girls of Lanark got into their starting positions. Being children, some of them were twice the size of others.

'C'mon, Ellie, get in there,' one enthusiastic dad encouraged his daughter.

There was a bit of jostling occurring among the children.

The MC reminded them: 'It's not a race. Enjoy yourself. Don't push anyone out the road.'

The weather was wicked but it wasn't having nearly as disruptive an effect as the BBC last year when they pitched up in Lanark to capture Whuppity Scoorie with their cameras. The BBC made repeated requests for re-takes. For the first time in its lengthy history, Whuppity Scoorie was performed not just once but twice in order to satisfy the broadcaster. Those children must have been dizzy running round the church six times.

The provost took to the mike and smiled down on the children who were getting impatient.

'I'm not going to join in,' he laughed, 'even though I have my Whuppity Scoorie ball here. But I'd like to swing it . . . ha-ha . . . Depends whit you're talking about . . .'

I doubted this was the proper arena for such innuendo.

At least it went over the children's heads. The church bell rang and the children were off and running. They were having a ball with their balls on string. In the olden days it was rolled-up bunnets instead of paper balls, but children rarely wear bunnets these days. Some of the bigger children were already lapping the little ones. One boy whacked another boy right in the face with his ball. Whether it was deliberate or not, I couldn't say. A boy of about four dropped his ball and, as he tried to pick it up, was knocked flying by an older boy. The victim hit the ground, got up again and carried on running. A few adults joined in, pushing babies in buggies. It was all part of the fun. One boy just gave up. Maybe his head was spinning from too much running around in circles. Two girls turned up late and joined in. Within minutes it was all over and the Devil had been given a right going over. He wouldn't be back in Lanark in a hurry. Not for another year at least.

There was further excitement for the children. Now it was time for the scramble. Clare said I should join in but I refused.

Not because I was ten times the age of some of these children but because I have bad memories of scrambles from my own childhood. Every wedding in Hopeman came with a mad scramble outside the church. We'd wait for the bride and groom to leave the church and climb into their big car. As it moved off, the married couple would chuck coins out the window. You'd get down on your knees and grab as many coins off the road as you could without having your hands run over by the wheels of the car. It was dangerous stuff, not least because you were all pushing each other out of the way to seize the most amount of money.

I'm still scarred by the memory of the day I spotted a shiny fifty-pence piece; the sheer amount of sweeties I could buy from Annie Stewart's with that shiny fifty-pence piece. I stretched out to reach it and a foot landed on my hand. It was a foot in a high heel and it belonged to an old woman in the village. I pulled my hand away in agony and burst into tears. The woman callously picked up the coin but didn't have enough time to put it in her handbag because my Auntie Minnie had witnessed the whole thing and stepped forward in a fury. I'd like to think that Auntie Minnie picked the woman up. She didn't, but she could have done because my Auntie Minnie is a giant. Instead she shook the woman and shouted at her and demanded that she hand the scramble money over to me or else there would be real trouble. Thanks to Auntie Minnie's intervention I had the shiny fifty-pence piece in my sore hand and the tears ceased. I celebrated by buying four packets of salt and vinegar Skydivers, two packets of Football Crazies, two Wham bars and ten flying saucers. I think I gave Auntie Minnie one of the flying saucers as a thank-you for sticking up for me. It was a positive outcome, but my God, scrambles could be vicious.

The children of Lanark were scrambling about now, grabbing as many pieces of silver as they could. Some of the kids looked delighted. Others looked quite upset. That's the problem with scrambles. It's the perfect environment for the playground bully – or the old woman with the pointy shoe – to have their way.

'Has anybody made a fortune?' enquired the MC. 'Thank you a thousand times for coming out. I'll see you next year at Whuppity Scoorie!'

The Provost then said something about keeping the tradition alive and added that he hoped next year the weather would be better. Well it couldn't be any worse.

Happy families started heading home. Whuppity Scoorie was over for another year. Clare and I were on the next train back to Glasgow. I think my wife enjoyed the outing. I sure know how to treat her.

Whuppity Scoorie is a hundred, possibly two hundred years old and may even be older than that. Nobody knows for sure and nobody knows what it's about. It is one of these lost-in-the-mists-of-time events. The locals can say what they like about it, because nobody can say otherwise. There's a real urge to keep it going. And it's the children that keep this quaint Scottish custom alive, with a bit of prompting from the adults. And there's nothing wrong with that.

Now that I was soon to be a dad, I might start up my own custom for my own children to pass down to their children. They could run round the block three times, with paper cutlasses, chasing the Burghead Ogre away. I'd call it Whackety Brocher. But I wouldn't have a scramble afterwards. Not that I'm tight; I just wouldn't want anybody getting hurt.

Wait a minute though. I didn't have any beef with the Brochers any more.

I'd better cancel the whole thing.

Kiss Me, Kate

– Kate Kennedy Procession, St Andrews –

Springtime in St Andrews. I couldn't have picked a better time and place. I almost went to the University of St Andrews to study algebra. But I changed my mind and went to Aberdeen and studied English. I'm still trying to figure that one out. Don't get me wrong, I loved my time in Aberdeen, getting rat-arsed in the Union, but I sometimes wonder what it would have been like spending four years in St Andrews, playing golf. Mind you, if I hadn't gone to Aberdeen, I might never have met my wife.

Clare and I were in St Andrews for the weekend. The baby was due in three weeks. This was a chance to enjoy some time to ourselves before the birth of our first child. We'd booked into a lovely bed and breakfast, round the corner from the Old Course. I was also fitting in another festival, which was taking place right here in St Andrews. It was shaping up to be a great couple of days.

On a beautiful crisp morning, beneath a clear blue sky, Clare stood on the 18th fairway with the final green and clubhouse behind her. I took her picture, thinking it would be nice for the child she was carrying to see their mum from this moment, one day in the future. I hadn't felt this happy in ages. Life was getting better again. I was getting on with it. I had to. I was going to be a dad. Clare looked wonderful standing there in the breeze. She'd make a great mum. I was certain of it.

We had been walking off the most magnificent breakfast. I could still taste the black pudding. In a couple of hours' time, the latest festival on my list, the Kate Kennedy Procession, would begin. The Kate Kennedy Procession is organised by the Kate Kennedy Club, run by St Andrews students. The stated aims of the Kate Kennedy Club are to maintain the traditions of Scotland's oldest university, to uphold and improve Town and Gown relations – that's the people of St Andrews and the students – and raise money for local charities. The Kate Kennedy Club carries out a lot of charity work, whether it's helping the elderly, the homeless, or working with drug addicts. The club also throws a couple of major charity balls during the academic year but the main focus of the Kate Kennedy Club – and the key reason for its existence – is the annual Kate Kennedy Procession.

This spring spectacle is rich in history and heavy on pageantry. It celebrates some of the prominent men and women who have been associated with the university and St Andrews itself. These figures are portrayed by the members of the Kate Kennedy Club and other students who tread the cobbled streets of this ancient town in costume. The crowds flock in their thousands to see a very popular and cherished tradition.

The main character in the procession is Kate Kennedy herself but not a great deal is known about her. Bishop James Kennedy founded St Salvator's College – from where the procession sets out – in 1455, intending it to become the focus of university life. He is buried in the College Chapel and in the steeple is a bell carrying an inscription mentioning that Bishop Kennedy had the bell cast and named it Katharine. The Bishop's brother had a daughter Katharine and so it seemed that Bishop Kennedy had named the bell after his niece. Over time, the legend of Kate grew and she came to be the focal point of a procession in which the students celebrate her life while welcoming the coming of spring.

By the latter part of the nineteenth century, the procession had degenerated into a disreputable affair. Students will be students and the university took a dim view of some of their shenanigans. Showing little appetite for rowdiness, the university banned the procession. It was curtains for Kate. Until, that is, she was brought back.

In 1926, two St Andrews students, James Doak and Donald Kennedy – a descendant of Bishop Kennedy – were inspired by J. M. Barrie's rectorial address on 'Courage' to form the Kate Kennedy Club and revive the procession with the support of the university's then principal, Sir James Irvine. The Kate Kennedy Procession has continued to this day, although not always with the complete support of the university.

In the procession, Kate rides in a horse-drawn carriage with her uncle Bishop Kennedy. The role of Kate is played by a first-year male student who only discovers he's donning the wig and the dress an hour before the start of the procession. Each year, nine first-year male students are invited to join the Kate Kennedy Club (whose membership never exceeds 60), after candidates are subjected to a series of interviews. The president of the Kate Kennedy Club plays Bishop Kennedy in the procession.

The Kate Kennedy Club has been the target of some criticism in recent years amid claims that it is sexist. The club is an all-male affair, although female students do take part in the procession, which involves around 130 characters. There's plenty of praise for the procession and for the club's charity work, but there's the charge of inequality from those who view the Kate Kennedy Club as an anachronism, an elitist organisation with out-of-date attitudes. The club does seem to get it in the neck from time to time.

I was approaching this seemingly closed society with an open mind. It was a club. Clubs, by their nature, have rules, and those rules are set by the members. I was going to enjoy the Kate Kennedy Procession and then chat to members of the Kate Kennedy Club. Clare was going to watch the procession for as long as she could stand it. Not because she was offended by the existence of an all-male club, but because she was nearly nine months pregnant and wasn't planning on standing in the street all afternoon when she could go back to a comfortable bed and have a lie-down.

My wife and I stood with the crowd outside the gates of St Salvator's College waiting for the Kate Kennedy Procession to begin. If the procession is partly about welcoming the arrival of spring, then spring was most definitely here to be welcomed. It was a perfect day in April. The students couldn't have picked a better one.

A lone piper played from the roof of the chapel. Then the gates swung open and out poured the history of St Andrews, of the town and the university. The eloquent commentary on the procession's characters could be heard loud and clear through the speakers and was a real bonus. Simply watching the procession might have been dull, no matter how impressive the costumes were, but listening to the stories of these characters made it a very involving experience. Clare and I were impressed from the outset. These students must have spent months planning this. We were rapt as we watched St Andrews' past and present combine. You could tell everyone else was enjoying it too. I can certainly say it's worth catching the Kate Kennedy Procession, and if you are blessed with a day like we had, with the sun shining, it is something memorable and something of which St Andrews can be proud – which it was, judging by the numbers that had turned out to see these students uphold their tradition.

'The history of the university is a common history,' began the commentator. 'Let the gates be opened and the procession begin.' First out of the gates was the university shield-bearer. Behind him was St Andrew, bearing the cross of martyrdom, the white saltire. It looked a tough gig to be dragging that about all afternoon. The crowd was told how St Andrew's relics supposedly arrived here during the Dark Ages, leading to the town's acquiring its name and Scotland its patron saint.

The characters passed thick and fast, in chronological order, a real array, some of them on horseback. There were politicians, scientists and royals. We encountered, for instance, William de Lamberton, a medieval church politician who became Bishop of St Andrews with a little help – it is said – from William Wallace, who saw Lamberton as a potential ally and supporter of independence. Lamberton rebuilt St Andrews Cathedral and played his part in the crowning of Robert the Bruce as King of Scotland. Then we were learning about the founding of the university, as another Bishop of St Andrews, Henry Wardlaw, walked past waving. He was the university's first chancellor. Then Pope Benedict XIII popped up. In the fifteenth century, he granted St Andrews university status and the privilege of conferring degrees.

Next up were the 'Martyrs of the Kirk'. Patrick Hamilton studied theology at St Andrews but was later tried for heresy. He escaped but continued openly to attack the Church and was condemned to death. In 1528, Hamilton was burned before these very gates. His initials in the cobbles mark the spot where he died. It is considered fatal to one's degree to step on them. You can cram as much as you like at St Andrews, but never put your foot in it by treading on the letters PH outside St Salvator's College.

We moved on to the Reformation and its leader, John Knox, who is said to have studied at St Andrews. And Mary, Queen of Scots who, with Knox hounding her, fled Holyrood for St Andrews, where her brother lived. Mary, apparently, managed to squeeze in a bit of golf while she was here.

I was approached by a drunk who offered me some of his port. 'Care for a swig?' slurred the man, thrusting his bottle towards me. 'It's 1891 . . . the best year.' I politely declined. He turned out to be a university dropout turned down-and-out. His name was Robert Fergusson. He had started studying at St Andrews but had soon gained a reputation for bad behaviour. He left the university without a degree, then found fame as a poet and was a big influence on Robert Burns. But Fergusson fell on hard times and he died at the young age of 24. His unmarked grave in Edinburgh was finally afforded the dignity of a headstone courtesy of Burns.

Fergusson staggered away from me in his red student's gown. When I saw him again half an hour later, he'd either lost his bottle or finished it. His hat fell off and he had trouble picking it up again. Then he leapt over a wall and was gone. What a curious fellow. What a fine piece of method acting. Mind you, he was a student. It's not the most difficult thing for a student to get smashed in the afternoon. Later on I saw Fergusson again, lying prone on the pavement. What a state to get yourself in.

At least the scientists were sober. John Napier of Merchistoun certainly wasn't stumbling about drunk as a skunk. 'Marvellous' Merchistoun – as he was known back in his day at St Salvator's College – was a brilliant mathematician. This is how marvellous Merchistoun was: he invented the decimal point! And he also discovered the common logarithm! When Britain was fighting Spain, Napier's contribution to the war effort was to dream up a mirror that would reflect the sun onto the Spanish ships and thus set fire to them. He even came up with a musket-proof chariot. Napier was suspected of being a magician. No bloody wonder.

It was Archbishop James Sharp I felt sorry for. There he was in his horse-drawn coach, his daughter Isabel by his side, both enjoying the procession, waving to the crowd, and every so often the coach would be held up by highwaymen in blood-spattered shirts and brandishing pistols. They'd drag Sharp out of his seat and onto the street and murder him before our very eyes, while his daughter looked on in horror. This happened repeatedly. 'Not again,' he must have thought as his life was ended for the umpteenth time. It was the Covenanters' fault. They sought revenge for Sharp's persecution of them. So his coach was held up between Edinburgh and St Andrews and Sharp was butchered in front of the hysterical Isabel. And, today, we kept getting gruesome action replays of the slaying. The only difference from the original crime was Sharp kept getting back up again and climbing into his coach. 'Put up more of a fight next time,' shouted one of the highwaymen on horseback, offering nothing in the way of sympathy for the sheer brutality that he and his fellow dandy highwaymen had just visited on Sharp. Towards the end of the procession, the poor man was being pulled from his coach every couple of minutes by his murderers. Still, it kept us entertained.

James Wilson walked St Andrews' streets without fear of being set upon. This local boy emigrated in 1765 and became a leading lawyer in America and one of the first Justices of the Supreme Court. He signed the Declaration of Independence and helped shape the American Constitution. James Wilson was one of America's Founding Fathers. Not bad for a Fifer.

Suddenly the procession ground to a halt. A wedding up ahead was causing the delay. The characters of St Andrews' past stood about chatting to each other until they could get going again. I wandered down the line until I reached the back of the procession and the carriage, adorned in flowers, carrying Kate Kennedy and her uncle, Bishop Kennedy. Kate – in reality first-year geography student Will Dawson – had flowing golden locks, and Bishop Kennedy – final-year history student and president of the Kate Kennedy Club, Will Roome – wore a big bishop's mitre. I'd spoken briefly to the bishop on the phone the week before and thought I'd say hello to him now while he was stuck in traffic waiting for the procession to get moving again. 'You always get headaches,' said Bishop Kennedy of the temporary hold-up. He then introduced me to his niece. Kate smiled bashfully. I asked the bishop about the interviews for the Kate Kennedy Club. What sort of questions were prospective members asked? 'Oh, you know,' replied the bishop. 'Things like "I Am the Walrus. Discuss."' Studenty questions then. The procession looked to be on the move again and I said to the bishop I'd catch him later, after he was done with the procession and showing off his niece. The bishop smiled and waved and they were off again. What a top bishop.

Clare and I witnessed a steady, um, procession of former university rectors. You couldn't miss Field Marshal Douglas Haig with his vast moustache. Then there was his successor J. M. Barrie. But for Barrie and his seminal rectorial address there probably wouldn't be a Kate Kennedy Procession today. You couldn't possibly have the procession without including the creator of Peter Pan.

I groaned when John Stuart Mill walked past. The liberal philosopher was installed as rector of St Andrews in 1865. I'd nothing against the man, other than the fact that I had to trawl through his book *On Liberty* at university and then answer questions on it in an exam. I wasn't in the least surprised to learn from the procession commentator that Mill gave the longest ever rectorial address at St Andrews. He spoke for nearly three hours. I hope listening to him talk was less of a struggle than reading his book. I had more fun reading *Ulysses*.

By this point the standing about was beginning to take its toll on Clare, who was starting to toil. She'd done remarkably well so far for a heavily pregnant woman. Now she was longing for the comfort of that bed. I offered to run to the nearest bookshop for her and ask if they had a copy of John Stuart Mill's *On Liberty* to help her sleep but she said she didn't need it. She was that tired. I told her I'd be back at the bed and breakfast within an hour or two. I waved cheerio to my wife and said hello to Rudyard Kipling. *The Jungle Book* author and confectioner of cherry bakewells was also a rector of St Andrews, as was comedian and author Frank Muir, fondly remembered as 'the hardest-working rector in St Andrews' history'. The student playing Muir sported a pink bow tie donated to the Kate Kennedy Club by Muir's wife after his death.

Fridtjof Nansen wasn't dressed for a spring day in St Andrews.

In fact the Norwegian polar explorer was ever so slightly over-dressed in his polar explorer suit. Nansen crossed Greenland from east to west on a pair of skis but was having trouble walking down the street today. Between St Andrew and his heavy cross and Nansen in his Parka-jacket-to-the-power-of-ten explorer suit, it was a toss up for which one of them was suffering the most during this procession. You couldn't see Nansen's face for his furry hood, but his leaden legs told you how he felt.

Nansen, however, wasn't walking as funny as John Cleese who, in 1970, became St Andrews' youngest-ever rector. Cleese's rectorial address on 'Cowardice' was a Pythonesque parody of Barrie's rectorial address on 'Courage'. Right now Cleese was running through his repertoire of Silly Walks for the entertainment of the crowd. He wasn't half bad at it either.

You probably won't have heard of Joseph Alistair Duthie, known by his fellow St Andrews students simply as Joe. Joe was captain of the cricket team, an accomplished debater and played St Andrew in the Kate Kennedy Procession of 1939. He graduated the same year with a first-class honours degree in Classics. The following year Joe joined the Queen's Own Cameron Highlanders. In the procession, the student depicting Joe wears the uniform of second lieutenant in Joe's regiment. Joe was killed in action on the 4th of December 1941. He is featured in the procession as a tribute to Joe and all the other St Andrews students who died fighting for their country.

Of course it wouldn't be a history of St Andrews without golf. Both Old Tom Morris and Bobby Jones looked very dapper as they swung their clubs and strolled around the home of golf. Old Tom Morris was born in St Andrews. He was a greenkeeper for the Old Course for many years. He was Open Champion four times. But Bobby Jones and St Andrews didn't hit it off at first. The American's first experience of the Old Course in 1921 was so bad he tore up his score card at the 11th and walked in. But he returned five years later to win The Open at St Andrews. Jones was that rarest of things, a golfer with more than golf on his mind. He held degrees in engineering, English literature and law. In 1958 Jones was granted the freedom of St Andrews, becoming only the second American to be given such an honour. Benjamin Franklin was the first.

The Kate Kennedy Procession snaked its way past the striking ruins of St Andrews Cathedral, where St Andrew's relics are said to have been brought. The cathedral was the seat of Scotland's leading bishops and Bishop Kennedy might have recognised it as he and Kate rode past, though he may have wondered what had happened to it. The parade of characters turned the corner and North Street stretched before them. They were nearing the end of their procession back to the gates of St Salvator's College. Archbishop James Sharp was now spending more time on the cobbles being murdered than he was in his coach thanks to the excessive attentions of the highwaymen. Last out of the gates and last back in, Kate and the bishop waved to the cheering crowd as the Kate Kennedy Procession came to a close. The students were back in the quadrangle shortly after four o'clock.

The huge cast gathered for a group photograph, the air filled with youthful excitement and a strong sense of satisfaction that the procession had been a success. Kate, Bishop Kennedy, the rectors, the golfers, the rogue Robert Fergusson sang and patted each other on the back. It was a genuinely happy scene. Bishop Kennedy's parents stood next to me. I asked them what they'd thought of it all. 'Fantastic . . . stunning,' said Will's dad. 'Couldn't have been better,' smiled Mum. I couldn't have agreed more and I knew a lot more about St Andrews than I had an hour or two ago. It had been an excellent history lesson in the sunshine.

The bishop was thrilled at the way it had gone – and a little relieved. 'It's been a year-long thing,' said the Kate Kennedy

Club president. Will was also nearing the end of his studies at St Andrews. 'I have three weeks left of tuition,' he smiled, 'which is a good thought and a slightly depressing one.'

The other Will, Kate Kennedy, still a teenager, made me feel very old. I was nearly twice his age. How could that be? My own student days had felt just like the day before yesterday, until now. Will was on a total high, having performed the eponymous role of the procession.

'It was a completely different experience from anything I've done before. It was really quite surreal. I only found out an hour before so there wasn't time for it to sink in. It is such a shock to the system. It was only really when I came out to the reception everyone gave me, in particular the members of the club. It was exceptional, a really warming feeling. And I think it underlines the camaraderie and the friendship of this club. This afternoon, the procession, it's such a privilege to be part of something that's brought so much enjoyment to so many people. One of our main aims is to promote town and gown relations and you can see on a day like today that we've been able to do this. And it is such an honour.'

I was introduced to Tom Kadri, a second-year student of international relations. Tom is vice president of the Kate Kennedy Club and was Marshal of the Procession. It had been Tom's task to ensure that everything ran smoothly. He could congratulate himself for that. When Tom was appointed Marshal, he had been handed a heavy file on the Kate Kennedy Procession. 'You get a file passed down to you,' said Tom, 'but that's only the tip of the iceberg. It's only really in these past three or four weeks, when things are more imminent, that you feel what this day is really all about. On a day like today . . .'

'Are you welling up?' asked the bishop.

'I must admit . . .' said Tom who was feeling emotional.

Kate came to the rescue. 'Leaving the quad, I had tears in my eyes and I really struggled to hold them back. And, in fact, they are almost coming back now.'

The bishop and Tom laughed.

'The meaning of this day is instilled in every Club member,' said Tom, who'd regained his composure, 'but, personally, I remember not truly realising until the procession itself. You hear the word "procession" and you don't really know what that means. It could mean anything. It could be a crowd of ten people or a thousand people. And it's when you come here today and see . . . students, definitely, but it's a town day.'

'We have three aims,' continued Tom, explaining the essence of the Kate Kennedy Club. 'Aiding Fife charities – not just raising money, but going out and helping them out – and then there is the town and gown, and maintaining tradition. Something I felt, going back through the Marshal's files, was that even in times of adversity, our argument for why it should stay the same – not necessarily all of it, but certain core aspects – was about maintaining a legacy.'

I wondered about some of the flack the Club attracted from time to time. David Borowsky, a financial economics student from western Massachussetts, responded. David had a very grand title. He was Keeper of the Costumes, the man in charge of the togs. 'It's a coming together event, is what it boils down to. Whatever press the club has got over the past few years, what the procession does is bring together the people of the town, the university, other students as they get involved as characters in the procession. Everybody just bonds around the amazing history and character of this town.'

'It's the tradition of the university,' added the bishop. 'It's very much a spectacle of the town. While there are students there who don't necessarily grasp what it's all about, it's the town people who have been living here for years that understand what the procession means.'

I asked them if it was possible for any male first-year student at St Andrews to join the Club, because another charge that's laid at the door of the Kate Kennedy Club by its critics is that it is an elitist society, excluding the majority of boys, as well as all the girls.

'Any matriculated first-year student at the university is invited for interviews,' said Tom. 'Something we try and do is to reach as many people as possible. Sometimes it's hard to let everybody know exactly when to apply but we try and raise as much interest as possible – and then you go through your two-round interview where you are aiming to show your enthusiasm for the Club, its aims and the history.'

The conversation turned to costumes. 'We had a new Field Marshal Haig uniform made recently,' said the Bishop. 'The university lets us store them all. Any character can be added at any time. You can propose a new character for the procession. It can be seconded. Often it's "What do they wear?" You don't want too many suits. We can drop them too. It might change by one or two. While we endeavour to fill every position on the day it's not always possible. My brother Tim was told at twelve thirty today that he was in the procession because we were one down. "You know you're in town? How would you like to walk around for a bit?" "What?"

'An important thing is that the life members of the Club keep coming back and staying constantly involved and they ultimately make everything tick. They are the ones you can go to when you're not sure about tradition. Even my costume, what bit goes on what bit? They've been doing it for thirty years and they make a massive amount of effort.'

'It's a double-edged sword,' smiled Tom, 'because then they hold the power to make you think you are forgetting things! I had the former Kates at lunch today saying to me, "You've got Kate's costume right? You've got that sorted?" '

'Oh, they got you with that?' laughed David.

'Yes. They were saying, "You're going to need to go and find it now!"'

The Kate Kennedy Club must take up a lot of their time, I said. What about their studies? It was a daft question to be asking a bunch of students, especially since I'd been one myself once, having a grand total of two lectures a week and still managing to miss both of them because they began at the ungodly hour of nine in the morning.

'What studies?' asked the bishop to laughter all round.

'St Andrews, four-year gap year, you can put that in!' suggested Tom. 'At the university you're pushing academics but at the same time, at the end of the day, you have a couple of hours' lecture a day and the odd tutorial. If you are not getting involved in other things I think you are missing out. And this is the best thing I can think of to get involved in. And things like this, with that comes better studies. If you are happier outside of the classroom, you are happier inside.'

They were certainly happy now. So what was next on the cards?

'We've got to clean up, sort out the coaches and then dinner tonight,' said the bishop.

My wife and I had been kindly invited to that dinner by the bishop but unfortunately we'd had to decline. For Clare, the thought of attending what was a formal affair, in evening dress, when she was nearly nine months pregnant, well . . . The better option for us was a quiet meal in St Andrews and a relatively early night, which is what we ended up doing, and it was nice.

The students of the Kate Kennedy Club had been nothing but courteous, generous, friendly and helpful. To me, they had a procession to be proud of. They had a keen sense of history and a strong willingness to maintain their tradition. They clearly loved their university and I'd enjoyed meeting them and being part of their day.

Happy Lanimers!

– Lanimer Day, Lanark –

Whuppity Scoorie hadn't frightened me off Lanark for life. I was back again. And no one was hunting down the Devil this time. The locals were pleased as punch. The whole town seemed delighted to see me. Everyone kept wishing me a 'Happy Lanimers!' I treated it like 'Happy New Year!' and wished them a 'Happy Lanimers!' back. I shouted 'Happy Lanimers!' until I got sick of shouting it, which wasn't quite in keeping with the spirit of Lanimer Day. My goodness, these people were happy. You'd think they were drunk. They couldn't have been drunk – it was monstrous o'clock in the morning. I'd got up at the crack of dawn to hightail it to Lanark. I didn't want to miss any part of Lanimer Day.

Mind you, getting up at the crack of dawn was a cinch these days. I was getting up at all hours. I was a new dad with a beautiful baby daughter, Isabella Rose, the happiest and sweetest thing that had ever happened to me. Mother and baby were fine. They were better than fine. They were amazing, and I was the luckiest man in the world. I wanted to spend every minute of my day with Isabella Rose. But today Dad had to be in Lanark.

As soon as I stepped off the train there were tell-tale signs that this was no ordinary day in Lanark. A pipe band tuned up – and perked me up – in the supermarket car park. I popped into the supermarket for a bottle of water and waited at the till behind a young piper buying a bumper-sized bottle of Smirnoff Ice. It's one of the best things for cleaning your pipes.

A man rode by on a horse. Not in the supermarket; I was outside again. The day had a big-day feel. Lion Rampants hung in house windows, something I usually associate with Scotland games. The chip shop was open. It was too early for chips (it was eight o'clock in the morning) but I went in and ordered a wake-me-up coffee and sat down at the Formica table. I studied the laminated Lanimer Day Menu. By the looks of it, I'd be back later on for my supper. There was no white pudding but the jumbo haddock sounded good. That's what I'd have, a fish tea. I'd never heard of a fish tea until I moved down to Glasgow. We didn't have fish teas in the north. Sure, we had fish and chips, but not fish teas (fish and chips, side plate of bread and butter and a cup of tea). King rib! I hadn't had a king rib in years. I never really knew what a king rib was, though it never stopped me ordering one. What is it a rib *of* ? Is it really a rib of anything? Whatever it is, it only exists in chip shops. King ribs are great.

A child wizard stared in the window at me as I drank my coffee. It was slightly unnerving. Then he became fed up staring at me and walked off. I hoped he hadn't cast a spell on me. Another boy, with a golden turban on his head, ran past, followed by a woman in a black cape, pushing a buggy with a baby caterpillar.

I rubbed my eyes and had a scan of the local paper. The letters page was dominated by a debate over a drinking ban. It seemed that there had been a move to ban public drinking in Lanark on Lanimer Day. Some residents had been shocked over the past few years to witness what they felt was excessive drinking on the day. By the sounds of it, there was a tension between the notion of a family day out and the reality of adults getting hammered. One worried reader recounted watching the Lanimer Day Parade with his three children and 'ahead of us were four teenagers, around fifteen years old. Three were carrying Buckfast, all four were staggering and swearing, and then one proceeded to vomit three times onto the road. You can imagine how the conversation turned from best float to "why are they doing that?" Unless the problem is addressed, Lanimer Day will become more known for its alcoholic rather than community spirit.' None of this sounded unfamiliar to me. It wasn't just Lanark's problem. It's a potential problem all over Scotland on festival days like these. Where there's a celebration, there's usually drinking. There's nothing wrong with a drink. But it really is about moderation, and I'm no puritan.

The Lanimer Committee wanted South Lanarkshire Council to close the loophole which permitted drinking in public on Lanimer Day. There was growing concern at the number of drinkers staggering around the streets wasted and ruining everyone else's fun. People from other towns were flocking to Lanark with their carry-outs. And there appeared to be a real problem with teenage drinking. Again, I wasn't surprised. Scotland is awash with alcohol.

I finished my coffee and went for a walk. I spoke to a man outside the Memorial Hall. I told him I was looking forward to Lanimer Day. He told me I'd already missed the best bit. He explained to me that Lanimer Day is part of Lanimer Week and that a couple of nights ago they'd had the Perambulation. The whole town had taken its legs to the countryside and inspected some stones. And I'd missed it. It's typical. I'm always the last to know when there's a Perambulation going on.

Lanark is one of the oldest Royal Burghs in Scotland. When Royal Burghs were created, the people of the towns had to check the boundaries every year to make sure there had been no encroachment by neighbours, and report their findings back to the Crown. Boundaries followed natural features like rivers or dykes. Stones – 'march stones' – were placed at points where the boundary departed from the river or dyke, or changed direction.

The inspection of the boundaries – ensuring that they remained intact and the stones hadn't been displaced or removed – was known as Riding the Marches. In Lanark, the checking of the landmark stones became known as Landmarch and eventually Lanimers. Of course, the exercise is no longer necessary. But that doesn't prevent the practice from continuing. What was once a routine duty has become more of a festive affair, a big song and dance made of it. Nowadays it is symbolic, about reasserting local identity. And it's a good excuse for a party.

The man outside the Memorial Hall reached into his pocket and gave me a medal. Not for missing the Perambulation, but for being here on Lanimer Day. I thanked him. I'd never had a medal before. Not a gold one, anyway. In a short time, the Lanimer Day Parade would pass the Memorial Hall. I walked further up the street to the parade's starting point. There was a silver band and I was treated to a burst of tuba and the belting of drums as the band warmed up. Now that was a wake-up call. The children of Lanark were getting ready for the parade. There were bumble bees, matadors, French children (you could tell by the fact they sported berets and wore strings of garlic round their necks), and I was thrilled to see a couple of Mr Men, especially Mr Strong.

I was once Mr Strong during Hopeman Gala Week – a long time ago, I'd like to point out. My dad turned me into Mr Strong. He put me inside a large cardboard box. It was painted red. There were holes for my arms and legs, and smaller holes for my eyes, so I could see out of my cardboard box. I wasn't sure about the red tights, but they at least gave me legs the same colour as Mr Strong. Dad stuck a green bowler hat (I don't think it was a real green bowler hat, more an approximation of one) on top of my head/cardboard box and that was me: Mr Strong. I think I came second. Another year my brother and I were entered together as Popeye and Olive. I don't see why I had to be Olive. Again, we picked up a prize but I was far from comfortable with the cross-dressing, even at that young age. I much preferred it the year me and Mark Fennell were Laurel and Hardy. Being the weedy one, I had to be Stan Laurel. I practised my girning face. I believe we finished first.

It's almost 20 years since Mark Fennell and Craig Fiske were killed in a car crash. Here was I just getting used to life without my dad, but I can't believe I have lived more of my life without Mark and Craig than I did with them. They were my friends. They'd not long left school and were making their way in the world. They were so charismatic, the pair of them. They'd be successes now, in whatever they did. They are never far from me. I don't forget them. And there are moments like now when I think of them and remember them, as they were, in the prime of their lives, full of fun, cheek and intelligence. It's not fair. It's really not fair. Part of me has never got over it. I sometimes feel guilty being here when they're not. I know that's not right, but it's hard not to think that way. I think of their mums and dads and brothers and sisters. This world isn't so well off without Mark and Craig.

Preparing for the parade, Mr Strong stood next to Mr Happy. I'd always found Mr Happy boring. He was more than a bit bland. Whereas Mr Strong, he ate hundreds of eggs . . . and that was just one breakfast. The eggs gave him strength, you see. He was so strong that when a farmer's field was on fire, Mr Strong picked up the farmer's barn and filled it with water. And guess what he did next? Yes, he poured the water on the field thus putting the fire out. Mr Strong wasn't just strong. He was clever, but not as clever as Mr Clever, who was one of the cleverest people in the world. My brother's favourite was Mr Bump, which was very apt, because my brother is very accident-prone. My brother and Mr Bump were always having accidents. I don't think Mr Bump ever swallowed his own tongue though. My brother usually got injured playing football. He's suffered 57 separate injuries on the field of play. He should really stop playing football.

The children of Lanark were blowing pretty bubbles in the air. Already barbeques were being lit in front gardens. It seemed a bit early for a barbeque, half past eight in the morning, but when you have a barbeque you can have a beer. It was fairly early for that too. A group of teenage boys strutted down the street carrying plastic bags full of Buckfast and Blue WKD. One boy was polishing off a bottle of Bud. I'm not sure if it was his first of the day. I was more surprised to see a pair of greyhounds wrapped in saltires. I once met a Rottweiler in a denim jacket, but that was in Stirling.

Yellow, green and blue bunting hung between the lampposts, the flags fluttering in the light breeze. It was a lovely morning. The sun had its hat on for Lanimer Day. People had put seats out on the pavement so that they'd have a prime view of the parade. There was also a great view of the surrounding hills. Lanark enjoys a great setting. They've been parading through these streets since the nineteenth century, although Mr Strong probably didn't feature back then.

I walked back down the road to the Memorial Hall to catch the 'Safe Oot, Safe In' toast that's a key part of Lanimer Day. This year's Lord Cornet, John Dickman, was on his horse. He's the Standard Bearer. He carries the Burgh flag. They've had Standard Bearers for centuries. Dickman was supported by his Left- and Right-Hand Men, also on horseback, and wearing red and blue rosettes, while the Lord Cornet's was white. They wore jodhpurs and bowler hats. They, and their fellow riders, would spend some of the day riding out of town to check the march stones. It's the element of Lanimer Day that's reminiscent of the Common Ridings that take place throughout the Borders. I'd be going to one of those in a couple of months for the first time. The 'Safe Oot, Safe In' toast – drams supplied – was given by the Provost. One of the Lord Cornet's men was on the orange juice.

Soon after that the parade began, led by the Lord Cornet. Behind him was a convoy of lorries-cum-floats with people in various states of fancy dress. Some in the parade carried branches of birch trees. This harks back to a dispute centuries ago between a local laird and the local people arguing for their right to cross the land. In the mid-nineteenth century, those perambulating were accused of damaging dozens of young birch trees and the laird decided that the people of Lanark should not trespass on his land. After years of debate, it was found that the laird had never really owned the land in the first place. So the tradition was upheld, the march stones were checked, the people walked where they wanted to walk and the birch branches were carried to show that the Lanarkians had the right to perambulate and so there.

Thousands of spectators lined the route. Friends were phoning friends to see who had the best vantage point. 'Have you got a spot?' The civic pride of Lanark came to the fore in the commentary over the speakers. 'Let us congratulate everyone who has worked to promote the festival. Let us sit back and enjoy the fruits of our labours. We're all on the edge of our seats, such is the excitement. Happy Lanimers!' I wished the woman standing next to me a 'Happy Lanimers!' and she wished me the same. I was getting the hang of this.

A man in an oxygen mask staggered down the street. He looked like he should have been resting up in the hospital. He was being chased by a nurse and there was blood on his shirt. Fortunately this was all part of the parade and not an interruption to it. '£5000 for a charity facelift' said a sign, another one proclaiming 'Dr Frankenstein consultant plastic surgeon on hire fae Wishaw General'.

It wasn't yet eleven in the morning but the Horse & Jockey was doing a roaring trade, judging by the amount of punters coming in and out of the pub. Every shop was closed apart from the off-licences. They couldn't afford to be shut on a day like this, when the booze was in such high demand.

A white vintage car crawled down the street. The car contained this year's Lanimer Queen. She was on her way to the Cross for her crowning. A temporary grandstand full of children awaited her. She was eleven-year-old local schoolgirl Sarah Smith, elected by her classmates. Every year a new Lanimer Queen is crowned. The first coronation was in 1893. She had her Chief Maids of Honour with her and the rest of her Court waited on the dais for the ceremony to begin. There were several announcements and plenty of cheering. The Lanimer Queen knelt to receive her crown. The band played 'Flower of Scotland', 'Scots Wha Hae' and 'God Save The Queen'. And as I watched, Elvis walked by. He stopped a lady and asked her for directions. Elvis was lost. The Lord Cornet rode off on his horse with the Burgh flag. The wheels of cars and floats crunched on discarded plastic cups.

I saw the first casualty of the day. A pale boy, fourteen at the most, slumped on a step, two police officers trying to wake him up. It was half past twelve. A group of young men queued at the cash machine. They already had a case of beer each. A teenage boy was on the phone: 'Wee Dazza's bin lifted. Ah'm sober noo . . . Ah need tae go, Mum.' Bits of birches lay on the road. There seemed to be a growing police presence. There were a lot of police in Lanark today. There were a lot of people getting steadily drunk. Some of the genial atmosphere of the morning had been lost. Some of the order had gone from the day. It was becoming more unpredictable. One boy approached another boy, one of his mates. 'Come on and we'll smash the bastard's face in.' 'How?' 'He's goan oot wi ma ex-burd.' What made this conversation incongruous as well as threatening was that mere yards away the Lord Cornet and his fellow riders were getting ready to lead the afternoon ride-out to check on the stones. I steered clear of the angry, drunk teenagers and struck up a conversation with one of the horsemen. He was Edwin Graham. He'd been Lord Cornet in 1997.

'Lanimer Day itself is really for the kids,' said Edwin. 'This ride-out we're doing is just a fun thing, after wandering around the streets all morning, which is a bit boring on a horse. We'll get a bit of a run at least this afternoon, a bit of a gallop. You need to be asked to be in the morning ride. I was Lord Cornet in 1997. I carried the Standard that year. It also involves taking it to the Border towns and visiting all their rides, because ours is an early one. Most of them are later on in the year. Lanark's quite an old Royal Burgh – 1140. Because the charters were given, you marched the border stones. We've actually replaced a few because they got moved over the years. We put them back where they should be. We'll check a couple of stones today to make it official. I've lived in this town since I was two and my father's a Lanarkian. That's what makes Lanark different from a lot of places: the tradition.'

I then grabbed a word with the Lord Cornet, Mr Dickman. It was strange talking to people when they were on horses. You had to look up to them. 'It's been busy, very busy,' said the Lord Cornet. 'I didn't know how much is involved when I accepted but it's been great, from one thing to the next. It's been brilliant. And I've been to one or two other towns already, where I've been absolutely welcomed. It's been a fabulous time for me. I hope the rest of the day goes as good as this morning.'

'Riders ready!' someone shouted and the Lord Cornet and his company of riders were off to check the stones, without much of a send-off. Everybody else was either in the pub or down in Castlebank Park with the funfair and Fergus the Pict, who was scheduled to make an appearance. There was a beer tent too. I didn't bother.

Back on the High Street there was a tidy-up operation with

rubbish being picked up and put into bags. The sun was beating down on Lanark. It was positively sweltering. There had been some kind of a fight outside one of the pubs and the police were taking down statements. Grown men (and women) were still pointing the finger at one another. The police told them to calm down. But when they've had a drink or ten, people find it difficult listening to the police. Away from these tense scenes, a young couple pushing a buggy stopped to speak to friends. The young couple had been in the park with their child but had decided to come away. 'We didn't hang about,' said the dad. 'There's a bit of an edge, folk fighting and all that.'

The rest of the afternoon passed without much incident – at least from where I was standing – and by tea-time the crowds had congregated at the Cross for the closing ceremony. 'Good evening, ladies and gentleman,' said the commentator. 'Have you had a happy Lanimers?' The crowd said yes and then the Dumfries Pipe Band was introduced. Out of the corner of my eye I saw a woman carrying a dead dog. I looked more closely and realised it was a toy dog, although life-sized and pretty realistic. The silver band played the theme from *Rocky*. I don't think the pipers would have managed that.

It had to be said that Lanark Cross, with St Nicholas Church, was the perfect setting for a ceremony such as this. The sun was setting and the mood was calmer. A Hare Krishna was darting about looking for people to shout 'Gouranga!' I'd seen her many a time in the centre of Glasgow asking shoppers to shout 'Gouranga!' Normally she was ignored or people ran away from her. Here it was different. She had a more forgiving audience in the shape of the merry Lanarkians. Some of them were happy to shout 'Gouranga!' as long as they could wish her a 'Happy Lanimers!' too. They were happy. She was happy. Everybody was happy.

The pipes started up and everyone turned their heads looking up the High Street. Here came the Lord Cornet with his flag. It was a stirring sight to a rousing soundtrack. 'Scotland the Brave' really got the crowd going. They were dancing in the streets of Lanark. But not everyone. A young girl sat slouched on pavement. She was starting to attract the attention of the police. Her friends were pleading with her to get up before she got in trouble but she was not for moving. She couldn't move. She'd had too much.

The riders circled the church. Whether they were chasing the Devil or not I cannot confirm, but it didn't look like it. They were taking their time. I overheard two teenagers with cans having a gentle disagreement. 'Lanimers. It's brilliant.' 'Naw, it's shite.'

The Lord Cornet dismounted and stepped forward to make his declaration. 'I'm bloody knackered.' Actually, he didn't say that. He said this: 'As Standard Bearer for this Royal and Ancient Burgh of Lanark, duly appointed and invested with the sash of office, I have the honour to report that, as charged, I have on this day and on Monday, Tuesday and Wednesday last, in the presence of many witnesses, inspected the March Stones of the Royal Burgh.'

He then left no stone unturned as he listed them all. 'The March Stone at Mouse Mill Brig . . . the March Stone in the River Mouse at Glenburnie . . . the three March Stones in the lands of Jerviswood . . . the March Stone at Oakwood . . . the March Stone at Leechford . . . the March Stone upriver from Leechford . . . the March Stone in the lands of Bonnington . . . Further, I have inspected the limits of the Marches along the highway, formerly the old Roman road from Lanark, to the boundary through Huntlyhill Mains Farm, from thence along the highway past the Turning of the Staff to Lanark Racecourse and from the Racecourse to the Cross at Lanark.'

He'd been very thorough.

'I have the honour to report that none of these stones has been molested and that there has been no interference with the ancient boundaries of the Royal Burgh and that I have duly discharged my duties in this respect.'

He received a big cheer for that and I was glad none of the stones had been molested. It might have ruined Lanimer Day. We were then treated to the Beating the Retreat and The Lament for the Lone Piper. Now folk were ready for their fish suppers. The silver band played The Proclaimers' '500 Miles' and a woman beat her man with a big birch outside a shop. Another woman was having some trouble finding her husband. 'There's an awful lot of wee baldy men,' she observed to her pal. She was right too. There were a lot of wee baldy men in the crowd. But which one of the wee baldy men was her husband? It was like trying to find a needle in a haystack made of needles.

On my way to the train station I got a high-five from a young boy who was either cross-eyed or was too far gone to focus. 'Heeey. Happy Lanimers man!'

'Happy Lanimers,' I smiled and high-fived him back.

Bad Satan

Brian and I were trying to remember a proverb about the Devil. We couldn't, for the life of us, put our fingers on it. 'The Devil's work is never done,' I said. '*A woman's* work is never done,' sighed Brian. I was confusing women with devils. It was an easy mistake to make. And it was typical of Brian to correct my mistake, since he's a teacher. In fact, I shouldn't be calling him Brian. I did call him Brian back in the opening chapter when he accompanied me to Orkney. And I've been calling him Brian in the first paragraph of this chapter, but, from now on, I'll be calling him The Manny Willox.

When I was at Lossie High, in the middle of an A-Ha explosion, my teachers were The Manny Barclay, The Manny Findlay, The Manny Knox and so on. And The Wifey Hepburn. Maybe I can start calling Brian The Wifey Willox. I'd better not. He'd batter me.

'A stitch in time saves the Devil,' said The Manny Willox. I knew what he was up to now. The Manny Willox likes mixing his proverbs. Mixing your proverbs is like mixing your drinks but without the disastrous side-effects, although within a couple of minutes of mixing his proverbs, Brian – I mean, The Manny Willox – had mixed so many proverbs he'd given me a sore head. 'Too many devils spoil the broth . . . People in glass houses shouldn't lead a horse to water . . . A rolling stone saves nine . . . A problem shared is a—' 'Brian, for Christ's sake, stop it!' But there was no stopping him. 'You can't teach an old dog and I'll scratch yours . . . Too many cooks shouldn't throw stones . . .

Fine hands for the Devil's work . . . The Devil finds work for idle hands.'

He'd got it, after all that. You had to hand it to The Manny Willox. He knew how to mix his proverbs and solve them. Mixmaster Manny Willox. 'Stupid fucking proverbs,' said The Manny Willox. He didn't mean that. I hoped to fuck he didn't use that sort of language in the classroom. Nah, I'm sure he didn't. The only language The Manny Willox speaks in the classroom is the language of maths. Although maths can lead to swearing.

We were havering and we were cold. We were halfway up a muddy hill in the pitch-dark and pouring rain. We were on our way to the Devil-burning but we were beginning to lose the will and had certainly lost our way. 'I think it's this way,' said The Manny Willox. I followed him because I didn't have any better ideas. It was the middle of July and the weather was diabolical. It was raining cats and dogs and farmyard animals. We'd had a few drinks back in town. To be doing that and mixing our proverbs was pretty reckless. No good could come of this.

We didn't have a torch between us. We didn't have a clue. It was unusual for The Manny Willox to come this unprepared. Sure, he was wearing the right kind of footwear and he had on seven layers of clothing but he might have thought to bring a torch. Normally, The Manny Willox is the most prepared Manny in the world.

Once, he was driving from Aberdeen to Elgin when he passed a fellow motorist standing in a lay-by with his car on fire. The Manny Willox stopped, pulled a fire extinguisher from his boot and put out the fire. Who needs the AA or the Fire Brigade when you've got The Manny Willox? The Manny Willox also stores a case of Red Bull in his car (in case he gets tired) and a dozen travel rugs (in case his car breaks down in the middle of nowhere and he needs to keep toasty warm).

I was disappointed that The Manny Willox hadn't brought a torch on a night-time hill climb. He'd let me down. He'd let himself down. The Manny Willox knew as much and muttered something like 'Neptune's fiery bollocks'. I didn't quite catch it what with the rain ricocheting off my ears and branches smacking me in the face. 'I should have brought a flask of soup,' said The Manny Willox. He had failed on yet another count. No soup.

Surely at some point we'd stop going uphill because we'd reached the top of the hill. But this hill went on forever. We came to a gate. The Manny Willox said it was a kissing gate. 'I'm not going to kiss you,' I said, making that quite clear.

We struggled on and finally we were able to make out the brow of the hill and a sinister silhouette. It gave me the creeps and rightly so, because it was the Devil. Lucifer himself was hunched and perched on a stick on top of a bonfire, which the natives were going to light shortly. He looked pissed off, did Satan. There was a cordon around him. In a while there would be a crowd on this soggy hill watching him fry. But they weren't here yet. At the minute it was just me, The Manny Willox and the Devil. The Manny Willox and I had somewhat jumped the gun. We'd set off far too early. Already we were at the scene of the Devil-burning ceremony, yet he wasn't due to be torched for another hour. In our eagerness to be here, we'd messed up seriously on the time front.

The Manny Willox and I stared at the effigy of evil and looked down to the lights of the town. Everybody was still in the pub. We should've still been in the pub, but instead we were up here. When we'd left town, half an hour ago, I'd asked a man in the street how you got to the top of the hill. 'You fucking run,' he'd answered. He was a bit pissed. We hadn't run up the hill – more stumbled really – but we'd still got here far too quickly. What were we going to do for the next hour? Mix proverbs? The

Torchlight Procession was due to leave town at ten o'clock. It was half past nine. 'It's half past nine, Brian,' I said. 'Oh well,' sighed The Manny Willox. 'We've got a good seat.' And we sat down on top of the dry-stone dyke with the Devil giving us evils.

'We could go back down for another pint and follow the parade up,' I suggested as the rain fell heavily and steadily. 'Nah,' said The Manny Willox. 'It's everyone else that's missing out.' Now that our eyes had adjusted to the dark we actually had a nice view of the town and the river and the hills. But the view could have waited. I studied the Devil in his red breeks. He was starting to look less terrifying. In fact, there was something vaguely comic about him. Not that I was laughing. 'What time is it?' I asked The Manny Willox. 'Twenty to ten.'

Innerleithen is a small and pleasant Devil-loathing town in the Borders, between Peebles and Galashiels if that helps. Nestled in the Tweed Valley, Innerleithen had made an instant and positive impression on me when I had arrived by bus from Edinburgh the night before. The Manny Willox had only joined me this morning. He had a fire to put out or something. The Manny Willox had driven all the way down from Aberdeen and, boy, was he glad to be here, catching a cold on this sodding hill.

The burning of the Devil – or Deil to give him his local title – is the culmination of Innerleithen's week-long summer festival, the St Ronan's Border Games and Cleikum Ceremonies, or SRBGCC for short. The Manny Willox and I had attended the St Ronan's Border Games that afternoon. I'd gone to watch the Cleikum Ceremonies the previous night.

Innerleithen is a town of myths, most of which the towns-people have made up themselves. The people of Innerleithen have plenty of imagination and they're not afraid to use it. There's a lot of claptrap, gibberish, balderdash, hogwash and rubbish, but the claptrap, gibberish, balderdash, hogwash and rubbish is for good reason. It results in a cracking festival that gets everyone involved and feeling proud of their town. So who cares if a lot of it is bollocks? Burning the Devil wasn't the half of it. They'd invented a whole pile of stuff.

Once upon a time – in the eighteenth century – Innerleithen was a bustling tourist resort. People travelled from far and wide to 'take the waters' at the mineral springs of this spa town. It mattered not that the water had 'the smell of an ancient egg'. The waters were famed for their medicinal properties and were valued as a treatment for gout, rheumatism, bile, scurvy and – most improbably – sterility. But it wasn't the waters alone that drew the crowds to Innerleithen. The people of Innerleithen showed the kind of marketing savvy that would make Saatchi and Saatchi proud.

The spark for the immense popularity of this little Borders town was a book written by Sir Walter Scott. And that book was *St Ronan's Well*. Scott was already a literary superstar when the novel was published in 1824. *St Ronan's Well* portrayed the well-to-do society of the fictional spa town of St Ronan's. The people of Innerleithen, eyeing an opportunity to put their little town on the map, seized on *St Ronan's Well* and declared that Scott's book was based on Innerleithen. It didn't matter if it wasn't. Whether there were elements of Innerleithen in *St Ronan's Well* or not, the novel quickly became associated with Innerleithen, whose inhabitants made a great song and dance about it. They had spotted their chance and they'd grabbed it. And it worked. The town was swamped with spa tourists and a pavilion was built to impress. Innerleithen's fame wasn't to be forever but it was good while it lasted.

The St Ronan's Border Games were first staged in 1827 to entertain the visitors and provide some fun for the locals. A key influence on the Games was James Hogg, the Ettrick Shepherd, a friend of Scott's, and whose novel *Private Memoirs and Confessions of a Justified Sinner* I read as a first-year student in Aberdeen. I remember enjoying it a heck of a lot more than Thomas Carlyle's *Sartor Resartus*. Scott lent his patronage to the St Ronan's Border Games and is said (by the people of Innerleithen) to have attended them. In any case, the Games proved incredibly popular. One year they were called off and special notices were posted at Waverley Station in Edinburgh, letting people know that the St Ronan's Border Games had been cancelled. Such was the influx of tourists to Innerleithen back then, eager to see competitors climb the greasy pole for a Borders bonnet and to watch more normal pursuits such as archery and wrestling and the 'Race Round the Town', which continues to this day. The Manny Willox and I attended the 181st St Ronan's Border Games. They've had a good innings so far and they still draw a crowd.

The night before the Games I had witnessed the Cleikum Ceremonies. This element was introduced in 1901 and Scott crops up again. The Cleikum Ceremonies were intended to introduce the young people of Innerleithen to the idea of St Ronan bringing Christianity to the area. In Scott's novel, a sign hangs above the door of the Cleikum Inn in the village of St Ronan's. The sign depicts St Ronan, with his crook, hooking the Devil by the hind leg. It is said in the novel that, according to legend, St Ronan, a Celtic monk, cast the Devil down to Hell by cleikin' him (catching him) by the hind leg with his crozier (crook). So, a century ago, the people of Innerleithen took a leaf out of the book of their ancestors, thought 'we'll have some of that', and conceived the Cleikum Ceremonies in which the Dux of the local primary school dresses up as St Ronan and good overcomes evil with the Devil getting what's coming to him on the hill on which The Manny Willox and I were hanging around, seemingly forever.

An hour before the Cleikum Ceremonies an elderly lady stopped me in the street. She was going to the Cleikum

Ceremonies herself and wanted to make sure I wouldn't be late. 'They open the door at half-six,' she warned me. 'You'd better watch coz ye winna get a seat when they shut the doors.' I promised her I'd be there in good time and would not run the risk of being locked out of the Cleikum Ceremonies.

In the meantime, I went to the pub. The barmaid was quizzing a punter about the Cleikum Ceremonies. 'Do you have to be invited?' 'No, anyone can go. It's boring, like.' The man took another sip of his pint and then changed the subject. Not everyone in town was going to the Cleikum Ceremonies.

On my way to the venue, the Memorial Hall, I passed a house with a painted picture in the window of St Ronan tripping the Devil with his hook. St Ronan wore his monk's robes. The Devil had hooves, a tail, red horns and a mullet – proof indeed that the mullet is the Devil's haircut.

The hall was filling up fast and I managed to find a seat. A lot of people ended up standing. The introduction was made to the 107th Cleikum Ceremonies. 'A very warm welcome to the hundreds of St Ronanites here tonight as well as the exiles and friends from other towns,' said our host. There was some piano playing and some choir singing. I felt like I was back at school. The scene was set and St Ronan and his brother monks took to the stage with solemn faces. St Ronan, played by Rob Lea, was presented with his crook – the Cleikum Crozier – by his predecessor. The crook was bussed with ribbon and the lantern was handed over to help guide St Ronan through the darkness. Cameras flashed and the commentary continued with messages about loyalty and respect. These young people, we were told, were the custodians of a tradition. Innerleithen's heritage was in safe hands. The previous year's Standard Bearer returned the Burgh Flag unsullied and untarnished (reminding me of Lanimers) and wished his successor all the best. The new Standard Bearer, Stewart Wilson, received the applause from the audience with his lass, Lynsey Thomson, by his side. Outside the hall afterwards there was a service 'For the Fallen' at the War Memorial. Then everyone strolled up a tree-lined path to the wonderfully situated St Ronan's Wells, where the Standard Bearer took some of the water and managed to keep it down.

The morning after the Cleikum Ceremonies, The Manny Willox and I visited St Ronan's Wells together. There is an excellent little museum and we met Christine who runs it. She spoke highly of the water. 'It's lovely. It's still got fantastic minerals. It's good for you.' Christine explained how Innerleithen was a place of little note until the mills came along. Innerleithen didn't have the past that other Border towns had. 'We had no history. We didn't have to ride the boundaries or anything like that. We had to make it up. A lot of it's a bit over the top. It was an opportunity. When Sir Walter Scott wrote his book, the town's folk said "That's us."' Christine invited us to try the water. The Manny Willox and I drank from paper cups. It actually wasn't bad at all. I'd been bracing myself, expecting it would taste horrible.

The Manny Willox and I headed off to the Games. They were well underway when we got to the field. Runners were circling the track and a lot of the crowd was either in or near the beer tent. I met Keith Belleville, who had been Games chairman for the past five years. Keith talked to me about Innerleithen's big week and the Cleikum Ceremonies. 'In essence, it's a Christian festival, but we don't overplay that. It's more the community aspect and involving the children. It's just gone from strength to strength. It's now a ten-day festival from Thursday to Saturday. It's not a Common Riding. The Common Riding was a functional thing to check the Burgh lands. Innerleithen was just a hamlet. Nobody was interested in the common land.'

Keith introduced me to the Standard Bearer, Stewart, who explained how he got the role. 'Previous Standard Bearers get together and bandy names about. "What do you think of so and so?", and they narrow it down to two or three. And then a member of the Games Committee joins in and might say, "Oh, wait a minute, he's an idiot" and gives his outside view. The final say is down to the last Standard Bearer, so next year the final say will be down to me. Becoming Standard Bearer, it helps if you are a well-known resident with a history of living in the town. My role primarily is to be here today to carry the Standard for this event. It's also to represent Innerleithen at other places, like Melrose and West Linton, Biggar, Duns, where they have Common Ridings and festivals.

'I took my drink of the water last night. It gives you health and vitality! It's a lovely wee ceremony. It's good, these things. I think they grow organically over the years. The bonfire, it's quite a strange tradition. It's one of the basic myths of good over-coming evil. This boy overcomes the Devil every year. It's hard to explain to folk from the city. I work in Edinburgh and it's very hard to explain to them what we do. "Aye, we burn the Devil." It's a wee bit weird to them I suppose, but I think it's nice. I'm extremely proud to be doing this. It's extremely tiring. I'm on a week's holiday. There's no way I could have done this week if I'd been working as well. You have to do a lot of socialising . . . late-night drinking. You need the rest during the day as well. It's been an absolute whirlwind of a week, to be honest, but I've thoroughly enjoyed it.

'These kind of festivals are a Borders tradition. I wouldn't say people in the Borders are prouder of their towns than other people, but certainly they identify with their Common Ridings and festivals, and Innerleithen is no different. At the same time, I think you'll find Innerleithen's festival is unique. It's got this novel centre of good overcoming evil. It's a total rip-off from Sir Walter Scott, to be honest. We just adopted it 200 years ago. But I'm convinced that this will endure forever, certainly well beyond our lifetimes. You can see all the mix of ages here today and that's what we need. That's what keeps it going. It's nice when the sun shines as well.'

I let Stewart, the proud Standard Bearer, enjoy the rest of his day and I went to speak to Alan Patterson. Alan is Keith's successor as president and chairman of the Games Committee. It was Alan who had introduced the Cleikum Ceremonies to the packed crowd in the Memorial Hall. Now he was enjoying the sun and Games too.

'My dad was Standard Bearer in 1962,' said Alan, 'and he was secretary of the Games for years. My family has always been heavily involved and I was Standard Bearer in '95. It's been a strong link. The whole community and family thing is a big part of this. One thing that's good about the week is the Cleikum Ceremonies involving the kids and instilling a sense of community in them. With the festival the demographic of the town has changed greatly in the last wee while. When I was wee there were five working mills providing all the employment in the town. Now there's one that provides employment for a couple of hundred people. So the whole town has changed. But even if it has, it still embraces the festival.

'You want to embrace new blood as well as keep the traditions and help the people who move into the town understand the traditions. Having kids involved helps that happen. If your kids are involved, you cannae avoid it, with people badgering you constantly to get involved.

'Outwith the Borders it's completely alien. I work in Edinburgh and you're trying to explain it to people and they're like "what?" They look at you. People at my work rib the guys from the Borders for having Common Ridings, but it's great. It brings the community together. I've been to two or three this year. When I was Standard Bearer it never stopped. Every weekend there is something on till the end of August. It's good fun.

'But today is what it's all about. If it wasn't for the Games there wouldn't be a festival. Almost two hundred years of history. Good against evil. It teaches them something – hopefully to have a wee bit of respect for the community. I would hope it continues without any changes. I've been around the athletics circuit and seen dwindling numbers and you sometimes think "what would happen if the Games died? How would we run things or change things to continue the tradition?" You walk down Princes Street in Edinburgh and you've got the Scott Monument, a statue to Henry Glassford Bell and there's one for the Ettrick Shepherd. These guys are literary heroes in Scotland and they are all linked to Innerleithen and Edinburgh's the capital city and you just think "you cannae let that die".

'World-famous punters came along a hundred and eighty years ago and for some reason picked Innerleithen. These were the guys who started it up and you think "how could you be responsible for letting that die?" You look at the history of this whole thing and think "my generation can't be responsible for letting this slide".

'It's a massive responsibility to continue these traditions. It's a huge pressure, but people give it their best and do a professional job to get this up and running. We're not famous folk. There'll no be statues in our names for years to come. But it's a fantastic thing to be part of.

'You go to Midlothian and West Lothian, with towns that were built around the pits, and they had their gala days and now the pits are shut down and they've lost their identities. The gala days still go on but they're not the same . . . But we keep churning it out year after year and I love it.

'I hope to continue Keith's good work and encourage younger guys to be involved and try to keep us going. I'll never want to see this die. It's just so good. I've stayed here all my life. I would never go away from Innerleithen. I cannae ever see myself moving away and I'd never miss the Games. If I was away on holiday, I would just sit and be a grumpy old git.'

'It wouldnae happen. You widna go,' chimed in his wife, Dawn.

Alan, like Stewart, was a young man with a sense of place. He was passionate about Innerleithen and about this week in particular. It was good to listen to someone who knew where he belonged. I thought about the geographical dilemma in my life. I loved Glasgow. I'd moved there for work and was still there twelve years later. But I missed Hopeman too. Sometimes I just wanted to step from the city to the beach, but they were more than four hours apart. I had days when I wanted to move back north, to be closer to my mam and my brother and sister. Maybe I would move back north with my family one day and give Isabella and any brothers or sisters she might have the kind of upbringing I was fortunate to have from my mam and dad. In a way I envied Alan. He wasn't torn between two places. He knew exactly where he was and he loved it dearly.

The Manny Willox and I sat on the dry-stone dyke on the hill, waiting for the people of Innerleithen to arrive and set fire to the Devil. At least the rain had stopped. We looked down into the valley and we could see flickering torches. The procession was on its way up. Soon we had company as the crowds started to arrive. There were people in T-shirts. I supposed the bonfire would warm them up. I thought about the manner in which they were punishing the Devil. Surely it suited him to be burned. Fire was his natural environment, wasn't it? Or was that just cartoons? Being engulfed in flames when you're the Devil would be a dawdle. They'd have been better off shutting him in a fridge.

Here came St Ronan and his retinue of monks. St Ronan moved close to the bonfire. He had the pleasure of lighting it, with a little bit of adult supervision. 'Burn the Deil!' someone shouted. Had the Devil even received a fair trial? I guess he was guilty of being the Devil. The bonfire was lit and the paraffin got it going. The flames soon tickled the Devil's breeks. He looked pretty annoyed about it. 'Burn the Deil!' 'Mair petrol!' 'Chuck it on!' Their appetite was insatiable. I thought about shouting, 'C'mon the Deil!' Not that I'm a Satanist, or that I wanted to stick up for the Devil, but just to be contrary. My friend Johnny Frank took the opposing view when I'd brought him to a bullfight in Spain. 'C'mon the bull!' he'd shouted from the stand. The Spaniards didn't understand Ayrshire, so Johnny Frank just kept shouting it. 'C'mon the bull!'

The bonfire was at its height and the Devil was melting. The Manny Willox and I were beginning to enjoy being up here. It felt like something out of the ordinary. It *was* something out of the ordinary. I watched the lights of Innerleithen through the smoke and the moon appeared. It looked huge. From up here it looked like you could reach out and touch it. Once the bonfire was petering out and the Devil was dust, the lot of us were all piped down the hill. The descent in numbers proved a lot easier and soon we were back in the pub.

It had been an unusual weekend, that's for sure, but on the whole, we'd enjoyed it. The people of Innerleithen, long ago, made something out of nothing and were determined to hold on to it. With people like Alan and Stewart around, I've no doubt they will be able to do that.

Innerleithen wasn't like some of the other festivals I'd been to, where the people knew what they were doing was important but maybe didn't know how it had come about. In this case they knew damn well how it had come about, because they'd concocted it, knowing exactly what they were up to. I had to admire the brazenness.

Maybe Hopeman could do it – pick a book and say 'that's us'. *Ulysses*. It's clearly a book about an ordinary day in Hopeman.

A Drunk Man Stares At The Thistle
And Scratches His Head

– Langholm Common Riding, Langholm –

It was a sultry summer's evening in Carlisle. I'd come down on the train from Glasgow and was on my way to Langholm in the Scottish Borders. Confusingly, getting to Langholm involved crossing the border and back again. Presently I was waiting on the 'emergency' bus service for the final leg of my complex journey. After recent heavy rain, part of the main road into Langholm had collapsed. Because of the landslide, we'd be travelling on the back roads. Reaching Langholm on public transport wasn't the easiest thing in the world, but I was in no hurry.

I hung about the bus stop next to Carlisle train station and eventually my bus turned up, a white mini-bus with a bit of cardboard on the dashboard telling me it was the No. 95 service. I liked their style. I hopped in. My only fellow passengers were a young couple from Galashiels, and their dog. We left Carlisle behind and soon we were passing one of those giant flashing road signs of the kind that usually tell you to watch your speed or warn you how tiredness kills. This sign simply flashed 'Common Riding'. It was effectively an advertisement for the festival I was going to.

After half an hour of rolling hills and fields of sheep, we approached Langholm. I knew we were approaching Langholm because of the giveaway sign saying 'Here Comes Langholm'.

Already I liked Langholm. They could have gone for a sign that said 'Welcome To Langholm' and been like most other towns, but instead they'd plumped for 'Here Comes Langholm'. Watch out! Langholm! I found humour and attitude in the sign. I decided Langholm was my kind of place and thought about the welcome sign to my own home village. On the edge of Hopeman the sign says 'Come Awa' In'. It's brilliant on at least two counts. One: visitors might not understand it. Two: those who think they understand it may feel they're being told to go away and come in at the same time. It's a very Hopeman sign. The sign as you enter Burghead says 'Danger: Broch'.

Entering Langholm it was immediately apparent that the entire town was in party mode. The streets were full of people. The old stone buildings looked beautiful in the sunshine. Langholm seemed the perfect country town. 'It's like Emmerdale,' said the man from Galashiels staring out the mini-bus window. He could hardly believe the crowds and said I'd picked a good night to visit Langholm. He fancied getting off the bus too. He didn't want to carry on to Galashiels. 'Have a good night . . . Have a good life,' he said to me as I got off the No. 95 with my bag. I wished him and his girlfriend the same and pulled shut the side door of the mini-bus. I'd set foot in Langholm for the Common Riding. Now all I had to do was find Nick. He was probably in the pub.

June through August is Common Riding season in the Borders. Common Ridings are all the rage in this idyllic part of the country where conflicts raged for centuries. Common Ridings are based on the ancient custom of riding the marches, inspecting the town boundaries, if you remember. Like with Lanark, it's no longer necessary to inspect the town boundaries in Langholm, but they can't seem to stop themselves. Why throw away the possibility of a good party? It's all ceremonial nowadays, of course, but in years gone by you had to be diligent. You had to jealously guard your land against covetous neighbours.

The Borders has a bloody and turbulent history. It was a much-disputed and ill-defined region of battles and constant upheaval, and plenty of plundering and cattle thieving by the infamous Borders Reivers (reivers being an old word for robbers). They were lawless times and today's Common Ridings mostly reflect this difficult past.

The first Common Riding of the season is in Hawick. It's a biggie and celebrates the capture of an English flag in 1514 by the young men of Hawick. Selkirk's Common Riding is a fair size too and is at least 400 years old. It dates back to the sixteenth century and is associated with the Battle of Flodden in 1513, when the Scots suffered a devastating defeat at the hands of the English army and King James IV met his death. It's said that of the 80 Selkirk men who fought in that battle, only one returned, carrying an English flag.

There's rivalry between the Borders towns when it comes to their individual Common Ridings, but there's a regional affinity too. You celebrate your own and you attend others. But there's nowhere better than Langholm (if you're from Langholm). There's no blood-and-guts story behind Langholm Common Riding, which began in 1816 with the locals checking their boundaries, having been awarded ownership of their land by the Court of Session in Edinburgh. The big day in Langholm is the last Friday in July, although the festivities run for almost a fortnight. Local pride is very much to the fore during Langholm Common Riding, when there is much going on in the Muckle Toon.

I'd known about Langholm Common Riding because every year without fail at this time my good friend Nick abandoned Glasgow for his beloved Common Riding. It wasn't something you missed if you were from Langholm. I knew two things about Langholm Common Riding: it involved lots of horses galloping and lots of beer being guzzled. I wouldn't be mounting a horse but I would be expected to make my way to the bar.

I stood in Langholm's Market Square in front of the Eskdale Hotel. Nearly every man but me was wearing a green tie and a green rosette. It must be the look. I phoned Nick. He was up the road, outside the Douglas Hotel. I was with him in seconds. He was with his brother Chris. Nick was sporting the green tie and green rosette combo. Green was the colour for this year's Common Riding. It is dictated by the racing colours of the winner of that year's Derby. Nick looked very smart indeed in his crisp white shirt and green tie. He was taking part in tomorrow's procession. I'd never seen him so dressed up.

'Aye, it's green this year,' said Nick. 'Some years it's been chocolate broon.' Chris was more casual in his black leather jacket and jeans. Nick introduced me to his brother. They were different but at the same time there was no mistaking they were brothers.

I'd felt scruffy and travel-weary but the mood was infectious and Langholm was already picking me up. It was a beautiful evening. I fancied a drink and asked Nick what he was drinking. 'Ah'm on the Tommy Todds.' I'd never heard of a Tommy Todd before. Nick usually drank Belhaven, or John Smith's, like my dad used to drink. So what in heaven's name was a Tommy Todd? 'Aye, it's a local drink,' explained Nick. Tommy Todd was a man from Langholm. One night in the pub he'd asked for a pint glass to be half-filled with ice and the rest to be made up with cider. Hence the Tommy Todd was born. And now pretty much everyone in Langholm drank Tommy Todds, especially at Common Riding time. 'Nae minny folk hae a drink named efter them,' said Nick. 'Mind you, there's McEwan's . . . Younger's . . . J. V. R. Tennent's.' Nick certainly knew his beer. I made my way to the busy bar and ordered a Tommy Todd. When in Langholm and all that. 'Tommy was in earlier,' said the barmaid. I'd entered a bizarre new world. The world of Langholm. The world of Nick and Tommy Todd. I was loving it already.

Langholm was reminding me of Hopeman, even though they're at opposite ends of the country.

I sipped my Tommy Todd and listened to Nick as he anticipated the thousands of people who would descend on Langholm tomorrow for the big day. 'Folk ye've never seen fir years. And folk fae Cumbria – they pile up tae get pissed. Ach, that's always the way. The police have a kind of stand-offish approach, but they're ayewiz nosin' aboot jist in case. A lot o' the Common Ridings are a closed shop but Langholm's different. The locals enjoy this – the night before. Before the rest wade in with their cerry-oots fae different places like the hinterlands o' Cumberland.'

Nick had a way with words. To top it off, he delivered them in his Langholm accent. Strangely, it wasn't far off the Hopeman accent. I'd been with Nick before when he'd been mistaken for a northerner. I first met Nick about eight years ago. We were both covering the Scottish Open at Gleneagles for different newspapers and Nick had offered me a lift back down the road to Glasgow. We went for a pint and we've been best friends ever since. Nick came to my wedding. Clare thinks he's hilarious. Everyone thinks Nick's hilarious. I now have a working knowledge of Langholm-speak. 'Yin mair fir the road' means one more for the road. 'Twee pints' means two pints. 'Thray o'clock in the morning' means three o'clock in the morning. You can see that I learned Langholm-speak in the pub.

From the Douglas Hotel – or the Dooglas – Nick, Chris and I wandered over to another pub with a wonderful beer garden, a courtyard with whitewashed walls and lots of flowers. We could have been in Andalucia, not the Scottish Borders. I went to the bar and bought a round of Tommy Todds and some pickled onion crisps.

On the walk back to Nick's later on, he started talking about his role for tomorrow. He was a member of the barley bannock crew. He would take his turn in carrying a pole through the streets. Attached to the pole would be a bannock and nailed to the bannock would be a dead fish, a salted herring. 'The saut herring's nailed through the middle like,' said Nick. 'Ah'll tak ye along tae Ian's the morn's morn an' ye can see it. Ian's the chief emblem-bearer.' The barley bannock is one of four emblems to be paraded at Langholm Common Riding. The other three are the spade, the giant thistle and the floral crown. But Nick was on the barley bannock beat. I had to see this.

I said to Nick how I liked the 'Here Comes Langholm' sign. 'Aye, watch oot!' he laughed.

Back in the house I met Nick's mam, Marion, and her grandson, Chris's son Wilf. Wilf thought I looked like Ronnie O'Sullivan. He's not the first. I once interviewed a footballer who, when I walked into the dressing room, exclaimed, 'Fucking hell, it's Ronnie.' I've had it quite a lot in my life since Ronnie O'Sullivan came on the snooker scene. Recently I'd had it on a train between Dundee and Glasgow. A group of kids in the carriage were sniggering and I was getting the distinct feeling it was me they were finding funny. They didn't say anything till I got up to get off the train and one of them piped up, 'See you later, Ronnie,' prompting fits of hysterics from his mates. I'm not Ronnie O'Sullivan's double – and I'm rubbish at snooker – but there seems to be enough of a resemblance for people to pass comment on it from time to time. Wilf's mum was back in Edinburgh. Chris said his wife had been to a couple of Common Ridings, but largely left him to it now. Chris though, like Nick, wouldn't miss the Common Riding. If you're from Langholm, you come back for the Common Riding.

I asked Nick and Chris about these Common Riding emblems – the barley bannock, the spade and the like. The spade was used for cutting sods from the ground at different points during the day. Apparently they drank whisky from the spade too. 'Pouring whisky doon the shovel . . . ach, this is difficult, this,' said Nick, standing in the middle of the kitchen, pretending to drink whisky from a spade. 'We should maybe use a shovel for something else . . . whit aboot diggin'?' This was the kind of baffling humour I liked. Again, it just reminded me of Hopeman and some of the surreal chat that's a hallmark of my village, the sort of light-hearted nonsense I'd grown up with, an appreciation of the ridiculous and vivid imaginations.

Though I was exhausted, I could have stayed up listening to Nick and Chris for hours. Chris entertained me with stories from a Mötley Crüe biography he'd read, tales of band members injecting Jack Daniels ('They forgot you could drink it') and phoning the hotel reception to ask them to get rid of the groupies outside their window ('But sir, you're on the eightieth floor'). I went to bed with a big grin and slept like a bannock.

At five o'clock the following morning – the last Friday in July – the brass band marched through Langholm blasting people from their beds. Luckily the band didn't come anywhere near Nick's house. I still had to get up fairly early but I was right as rain. The Tommy Todds hangover never materialised. On our way over to Ian's house Nick described the technique of carrying the barley bannock through the streets of Langholm. 'Turn and twist,' said Nick. 'It's quite baffling.' I was looking forward to seeing him in action. Ian and the rest of the barley bannock crew were waiting out in the garden, wearing their white shirts and green ties. 'The fish has taken a wee bit,' said one of the crew. I stared at the fish, nailed to the bannock. The fish was quite dead.

Ian explained the reason for the bannock's inclusion as an emblem in Langholm Common Riding. 'Well, the bannock was jist traditional fare in days gone by, ye ken. It was all people could afford. There wisna pizza in them days. The fish was jist a cheap relish to put on the top o' the bannock to make it a wee bit tastier. It's supposed tae be sauted herring but ye can hardly get sauted herring now. It's jist a herring. Ah'd a real battle tae get that on. The fish pit up a wee bit o' resistance.'

'Aye it'll be stinkin the day,' said Nick, checking out the fish and then turning to his fellow crew members. 'Fair bit o' seepin last night, eh? Ye need a wee bit o' ruggedness, divin ye?' I'd no idea what he was talking about.

Ian gave me his views on Langholm Common Riding. 'The likes o' Hawick and Selkirk celebrate battles. Oor Common Riding, we're riding the Common Moss to depict our boundaries. It's completely different frae Hawick and Selkirk. Selkirk's Flodden. Hawick is aboot a' these young men that went tae smash the English. Thir a' good in their ane way.' 'Aye, they're a' different', agreed Nick. 'Langholm's quite an open yin. Fowk jist pile in.'

I left the barley bannock crew to it so that they could get ready for their day. I'd arranged to meet Nick's mum at a sundial in front of a café. It was recommended as a spot for watching the start of the Common Riding. A huge crowd had gathered in the Market Place but I managed to find Nick's mum without too much bother. Nick's directions had been spot on.

The Common Riding's officiating magistrate made his opening statement from the podium. He articulated that the Common Riding was not only important for the people of Langholm but Langholmites everywhere, especially the exiles – like Nick and Chris – who had made their way home to be with family and friends. 'For those unable to make the journey, we can be sure that, wherever they may be, their thoughts will be here in this historic Market Place of ours. This is a day of emotion, of rekindled friendship and new friendship, of family reunions, but, above all, it is a day of celebration and – at times – the occasional tear. For first-time visitors and those who return year after year, it is a day not to be missed – despite the threat of landslides and other natural disasters. Work has been completed and life can return to normal.'

He then congratulated this year's Cornet, Simon Richardson – flanked by his right- and left-hand men – on fulfilling his ambition to achieve the highest honour Langholm could bestow on him. Simon was to be entrusted with the Burgh flag and was asked to carry it aloft with honour and dignity so it could be seen by all. After completing his duties as Cornet, he was to return the flag unstained and unsullied. 'For Simon,' continued the officiating magistrate, 'there will never be a day like it.' The Cornet eventually received the Burgh flag after several attempts were made to pass it to him while his horse lurched.

The procession began round the town with the band playing. I walked with Nick's mum to the bridge over the River Esk where she stood every year waiting for Nick and the rest of the procession to march back into town. I was introduced to more of Nick's relatives on the bridge. 'We're aye here,' said Nick's mum. 'We always meet up.' Nick's mum told me how Nick got involved with the task of carrying the barley bannock. 'We were neighbours of Sporty – Ian – and when they were little Christopher was the barley bannock man. He wanted to do it. They got in to watch it getting nailed on. They grew up with it. Nick was keen and Sporty asked him if he wanted to do it and he's been doing it ever since.'

We gazed down the street from the bridge. The procession was coming closer, with the barley bannock crew leading the way. 'Where's Nick?' his mum asked. As they got nearer still, she spotted him. 'He's on the end. He's got the swagger,' she said proudly. Nick certainly did have the swagger. I'd witnessed him move on the dance floors of Glasgow, but this was different. I'd never seen him twirl a pole with a dead fish on the end of it.

The whole town – emblem-bearers and all – returned to the Market Place for the first Crying of the Fair at nine o'clock. The Crying of the Fair falls into three parts. The first part calls upon the people of Langholm to go out in defence of their rights. The

Fair Crier, Rae Elliot, bawled his speech from the back of a horse. He ranted and raved in a broad brogue and it was all very dramatic. It was a mightily impressive performance. 'His dad and granddad did it before him,' whispered Nick's mum as Rae shouted himself hoarse on top of the horse.

Now, Gentlemen, we're gan frae the Toun

And first of a' the Kil-Green we gan' roun'; It is an ancient place where clay is got, And it belongs tae us by Right and Lot . . .

The Fair Crier held everyone's attention. It was mesmerising.

The next part of the Common Riding was even more stunning. The Kirk Wynd was packed with excited onlookers waiting for the hundred-or-so horses to gallop up the unbelievably steep hill, the epic charge led by the Cornet and the Burgh flag rippling in the breeze. This is the defining moment of Langholm Common Riding and it felt familiar to me although I was witnessing it for the first time. Perhaps I had seen a clip of it on the telly once or a picture in the paper. I couldn't believe how effortlessly they charged up that hill with the loud clattering of hooves. It almost took your breath away. I was standing with Nick's mum and Chris and Wilf, trying to keep my footing on the grass slope, and I was lost for words. The stampede up the Kirk Wynd was something special. And I'm not even that into horses.

The riders were off up to the Common Moss to check the boundaries. Some of the crowd started following up the trail to the top. Nick's mum said there was a nice view from up there and I decided I should check it out for myself. It would do me good to stretch my legs and get some exercise for a change. I ended up stretching my legs to the point they almost gave up on me. I underestimated both the climb and the heat.

It started out alright, with children skipping about and picking berries, parents chatting. I was feeling the benefits of a leisurely walk with the sun on my back. Then it became more of an ascent, the top of the hill within sight, but never seeming to get any closer. I started to struggle. My legs were weakening and I began cursing like Dick Dastardly's Muttley. Maybe I could get a lift back down on a horse. Perhaps there was a bar at the top and an outdoor swimming pool, one of those infinity pools. Last night's Tommy Todds were telling on me. I was sweating cider.

I finally conquered the hill over Langholm and basked in the welcome breeze, looking down on the town. The view was as good as Nick's mum said it was. You could see for miles, especially on a day like this. Over the back of a stone dyke there was nothing but wilderness. There were maybe thirty people on the hill, none of them looking as knackered as I felt. I looked over the dyke and saw a flag in the distance. It was the Cornet and his fellow riders. They'd checked their boundary stones and were making their way towards us. It was an awesome image, watching these horses coming over the moor. When the riders reached us there was the ceremonial cutting of the sod with the ceremonial spade. Then it was back down the hill. It was rough coming down too. It was like 'Kick Start' without the motorbikes. I was also freaking out a little about the horses. They're bigger than us. The sun was unrelenting. I was beginning to wilt again. A man in front of me had another problem. 'I'll tell you something,' he confessed to his friend, 'I've got a sweaty arse.' There was a group of men with a giant basket of salted herring. Everyone was sticking their hands in and grabbing some of the fish. What the heck, I joined in. It tasted good, but now I was even thirstier. I probably needed some water, but I knew I'd be having a Tommy Todd. Maybe I'd have a glass of water then a Tommy Todd. That could work.

I was back in the Market Place in time for the second Crying of the Fair. The Crier sounded as furious as he had last time. You couldn't take your eyes of him as he stood on the back of the horse, yelling at us.

Now, Gentlemen, we hae gane roun' oor hill,
So now I think it's richt we had oor fill
O' guid strang punch – twould mak us a' tae sing,
Because this day we have dune a guid thing;

For gangin' roun' oor hill we think nae shame,
Because frae it oor peats and flacks come hame;
So now I will conclude and sae nae mair,
And gin ye're a' pleased I'll cry the Langholm Fair.

He wasn't finished yet. He let out a blood–curling roar as his eyes bulged.

Hoys yes! That's ae time,
Hoys yes! That's twae times
Hoys yes! That's the third and the last time.

And that was that. Phew! He thoroughly merited his three cheers and the band played 'Auld Lang Syne'. The spade was in the air and . . . what the hell was that? It looked like a thistle but it was the size of a horse. It was the giant thistle, the fourth emblem of the Langholm Common Riding. The words 'giant thistle' would indicate that it was, well, a giant thistle, but this thing was *gigantic*. I had no idea thistles could grow to such a massive size. It was a freak thistle. How on earth had I missed it until now? I must have been too busy watching Nick twirling his fish on a pole. There he went again. 'He's a massie twirler,' said his mum. He was that. Nick was born to twirl a fish on a pole.

A short while later we were faced with the third and final Crying of the Fair. The first two had been performed brilliantly but, even still, this last was by far the best. The Fair Crier was on his high horse and he let us have it.

So now I think it's right we had our fill o' guid strang punch,
Because this day we did a good thing fir doddin roon the hill . . .

I almost did myself some ill doddin roon that hill.

I'll cry the Langholm Fair . . .

Here we go.

Hoys yes! That's ae time,
Hoys yes! That's twae times
Hoys yes! That's the third and the last time.

But he wasn't finished yet. Oh no.

This is tae gie notice that there's a muckle Fair tae be hadden
in the muckle toon o' Langholm on the fifteenth day o' July . . . auld
*   style . . .*

I'd thought 'auld style' was simply Nick's catchphrase. Clearly it
was a Langholm thing.

. . . and a' land-loupers and dub-scoupers, and gae-by-the-gate
swingers, that come to breed hurdums or durdums, huliments or
buliments, hagglements or bragglements . . .

He'd lost me there.

. . . or come here to molest this public fair, they shall be ta'en by order
of the Baillie and Toon Cooncil, and their lugs shall be nailed to the
tron wi' a twalpenny nail . . .

That seemed a bit much.

. . . and they shall get doon on their bare knees and pray, seeven times for the king and thrice for the muckle Laird o' Ralton, and pay a groat tae me, Jamie Ferguson, Baillie o' the aforesaid Manor and I'll away hame and hae a barley bannock and a saut herring tae ma denner by way o' auld style!

Auld style! Brilliant! He'd got it all off his chest and he was cheered off his horse.

Moments later I got a tuba right in my ear for standing on the edge of the crowd and not paying attention as the brass band walked by. It took me a while to recover. My ears had already been ringing after the Fair Crier. If ever there was a time for my first Tommy Todd of the day it was now. I went back to the scene of my first ever Tommy Todd: The Dooglas.

'Is that you back in fir yer Tommy Todd?' asked the barmaid, remembering me from last night. I nodded sheepishly and mumbled that it was slightly earlier than I would normally have a cider. Not that I normally drank cider. 'Aye, cider for break-fast,' she said. 'Ya canna beat it.' After my Tommy Todd I toddled off to the newsagent's to buy a paper and then I bought a bottle of water from another shop across the road. The same man served me in both shops, even though it had taken me about five seconds to walk between them. It did not compute. It was as confusing as the giant thistle. I hoped my top-up of Tommy Todd wasn't responsible, or I'd be spending the remainder of the day in a world that made no sense. I sat down for a minute and tried to regain my composure. I had a look at the paper.

A list of exiles ran the length of a page, Langholmites who had returned for the Common Riding. There was also a fascinating feature that flashed back to 1848 when local ministers had written to the paper expressing their concerns over the Common Riding. They had no beef with tradition but took a dim view of 'the improper use of intoxicating liquors, scenes of rioting, profane swearing, indecent language and often indecent conduct'. The clergymen warned that 'people were putting themselves in the hands of temptation' and the dog-collars dismissed the Crying of the Fair as 'buffoonery' of the highest order. I thought that was a bit harsh. It was ministers who had tried to put a stop to The Clavie. What's wrong with burning things? What's wrong with a bit of buffoonery? I like to think that if you want to caper you should be allowed to caper, within reason. Otherwise life can be a bit dull.

I got up and tried to walk again, wary of the universe around me, and paused at a sign in the baker's window. 'Muckle sausage rolls 90p. 5 for £4.50. Bargain.' The cunning baker was trying the same trick with his pies. 'Pies a pound. 3 for £3. Bargain.' Reading about all these bargains was making me hungry. A policeman walked past and was lucky enough to be wolf-whistled at by an amorous lady across the road. 'Eeh . . . get yer handcuffs oot!' She loved a man in uniform. With handcuffs.

I then saw a remarkable thing. A man standing in the street eating a fish supper. Nothing unusual in that, you might think. Except that the fish supper was on the pavement and the man was standing up. Each time he fancied a bit of fish he'd bend down, pick it up and eat it. He did this repeatedly – pavement, mouth, pavement, mouth. His technique was excellent except the scoffing of the fish supper off the pavement became more complicated when his mobile phone rang, but he answered it and held a conversation while bending down to pick flakes of fish off the pavement. Man Eating Fish Supper Off Pavement (While Answering Mobile Phone) is the best piece of street theatre I have ever seen. He should be touring the country with that back-bending act. Instead of giving him money the public would buy him fish suppers. While I caught Man Eating Fish Supper Off Pavement (While Answering Mobile Phone) I missed the Lord Cornet and his fellow riders crossing the River Esk on their horses. Well you can't see everything.

We were back in the Andalucian courtyard, me, Nick, Chris and their mum. Nick was taking a well-earned rest from twirling a pole with a dead fish for the entertainment of the general public. I asked about the state of the fish. 'It'll be stinkin' now,' said Nick. 'The guts are comin oot an a'.' Everyone in the courtyard – bar me, because I didn't know the words – started singing 'The Rose of Allandale':

> *By far the sweetest flower there,*
> *Was the Rose of Allandale,*

I tried my best to join in, but I enjoyed listening to Nick, his mum and his brother. It was heart-warming. They sounded good, too. Having a good time was second nature to the locals of Langholm.

> *Had fate not link'd my lot to hers,*
> *The Rose of Allandale.*

Nick finished with a flourish, chipping in with a harmony, providing a counterpoint to his mum's sweet singing. One minute he's showing off with his rotting fish on a pole and the next he's showcasing that fine baritone of his. He's a man of many talents, is Nick. 'Aye, it's jist good honest local scenes,' he smiled. I felt privileged being part of this scene. Family and friendship were firmly to the fore.

It was my turn to get the Tommy Todds. The bar staff were frantically scooping ice into pint glasses. They must have had an iceberg in the back for all the Tommy Todds they were serving on such a hot and busy day. 'Aye, you need a lot o' ice on a hot Common Riding day like this,' said Nick, tasting his Tommy Todd. 'If ye stop, it's fatal.'

Nick suggested popping back to his for some lunch. 'We'll

waddle doon the waterside wi' oor Tommy Todds,' he said. Off
we waddled, taking great care in sidestepping the hills of horseshit strewn across the street. It was a minefield of horse manure.
'It's the acceptable face o' faeces,' commented Nick. 'It's a gran'
smell. There's that carefree attitude towards it. It's jist horseshit.
The boys who clean the streets dae a remarkable job ince folk
have fucked off. Ye come back the morn an' it's clean.'

We compared our mornings. I told Nick about my walk up
the hill. 'It'd be quite nice up there far fae the madding crowd.' It
was nice. It was just the getting there that was monstrous. I asked
Nick about the monster thistle. They'd only cut it out of the
ground that morning. 'Aye, they keep it right till the last minute,
keep it fresh.' Nick had enjoyed his morning in the limelight and
sunlight. 'There's nothing like a good perambulation.'

After gorging on the super spread of lunch that Nick's mum
had left us, Nick and I went to the Castleholm for the rest of the
afternoon, where there was athletics and Highland dancing. As
well as a well-stocked and well-attended beer tent. Over a beer –
we were taking a break from the Tommy Todds – Nick
introduced me to one of his best friends from school, Gizzard.
Fortunately for Gizzard, that wasn't his real name. It was a
nickname, picked up during their school days together. Nick
tried to explain. 'Ah think we must have had a nature class. Birds
have gizzards. Robin's got a gizzard.' Which is pretty much how
nicknames materialise at school, the randomness of it, although
I'd never met anyone called Gizzard, until now.

Gizzard lives in London but if he lived in Lima he'd still make
it back to Langholm for the Common Riding. Nick told Gizzard
that I'd gone up the hill earlier. 'Have ye been up yersel since ye
came back?' Nick asked Gizzard. 'Only on a bloody horse this
morning,' replied Gizzard, who had followed the Cornet up the
Kirk Wynd. It had been no bother getting up that steep hill.
'They can do anything they bloody want, horses,' said Gizzard.

'It's a good adrenalin rush. At the bottom, you hold back and the horse wants to gallop. You try to get a straight run.' Gizzard's been going up the Kirk Wynd on a horse for twelve years.

The three of us watched a spot of Cumberland wrestling – grown men grappling with each other and trying to unbalance their opponent through any trick but kicking. If any part of one of them touched the ground – apart from their feet, obviously – then that was it. If they both took a tumble, the last man to hit the ground was declared the winner. Cumberland wrestling is like some curious dance involving strength and trickery. It looked quite ridiculous. 'It's a legitimate drunken brawl,' said Nick, who started shouting random advice to the wrestlers. 'Mind the rules, boys!' 'Have a wrestle!' A local wrestler was flying the flag for Langholm. He outfoxed his opposite and won through to the next round. The next bout looked like a real mismatch, a man the size of a house taking on a boy the size of a wendy house. 'You'll break his bloody back,' Nick scolded the giant. Surprisingly though, the scrawny guy won. He was never going to win in the brute-strength stakes but he'd shown more agility. It was a victory for the wee man. 'That's a turn up for the books,' exclaimed Nick.

The next match-up pitted a man in full wrestling gear against a man in jeans. 'Ye widna wint tae lose tae somebody in jeans,' said Nick. The man in jeans was soon flat out on the ground. Other fights were epics. 'It's like the Battle of Stalingrad,' said Nick. 'It's ridiculous when ye think aboot it.' Nick stopped commenting and started presenting the action, in the voice and style of David Attenborough. 'And here . . . we see the drunken wrestlers . . .'

We left the Cumberland wrestling and returned to the beer tent. I had a good chat with Gizzard about the Common Riding and its meaning in his life and why he was always here, without fail. As far as Gizzard was concerned, the Common Riding is less about checking boundaries than catching up with family and friends. 'It's as much about that as anything else. Close bonds, reflection, vodka lemonade.'

Nick had just asked him what he wanted to drink. Gizzard continued while Nick got the order in.

'It's about emotion. Friends that have died. People that aren't here, that are missing. That's the importance of it.'

Gizzard's words resonated. My dad was never far away, but I thought of Nick's dad, too. I'd never met Nick's dad, who had died a few years ago. A large part of Nick's Common Riding now – and his mum's and brother's – would be about what Gizzard was talking about, remembering those who are dearest to you.

Hopeman had no Common Riding, but a few weeks ago there had been a big wedding. My brother had got married. I was the best man. My sister was a bridesmaid. Our mam, the mother-of-the-groom, was there. But there was no father-of-the-groom. It was an amazing wedding, an incredibly happy wedding. Clare and I had two-month-old Isabella with us. She was a hit, of course, the baby at the wedding. But there were tears too. We were able to celebrate, but always remembering, thinking about that great man and just wishing he was there also, mostly for my brother, but for all of our sakes.

I returned to the Common Riding. Gizzard was talking. 'Most of the songs are about exiles, about coming back. It happens naturally. You just do what you do. The day's not long enough. Somebody said to me the day's getting shorter.'

'Common Riding measures.' Nick was back with some generously poured drinks.

I said to Gizzard that I'd developed a taste for the Tommy Todds.

'Per head of population,' he said, 'there's more Strongbow sold in this town than anywhere else. I say the marketing bods must be looking at the sales figures and Langholm's off the chart. They could advertise on the marquee tents but they don't need to.'

'Cider coats yer teeth,' chipped in Nick.

Gizzard wanted to talk about Neil Armstrong. 'He went to the moon and then he came to Langholm.' The astronaut came to Langholm – which is Armstrong country – in the 1970s. The first man on the moon became a free man of Langholm. 'His picture hangs in the town hall,' said Gizzard. 'He said he'd come back. But I don't think he has.'

'My mither's an Armstrong,' said Nick.

Then there was the Monkee who came to Langholm for the fishing. 'Mickey Dolenz from The Monkees came over in the sixties,' said Gizzard. 'He wanted to go trout fishing. It's good fishing here, lots of people pay lots of money for it. Somebody took him fishing and said, "Here Mickey, ye've got an affa skinny erse."'

From Neil Armstrong of the moon to Mickey Dolenz of The Monkees . . . to God.

'God's a Langholm man,' said Gizzard, proudly surveying the bucolic scene before us.

I felt the same way. Not about Langholm – the Muckle Toon's lovely – but the way Gizzard felt about Langholm, I felt about Hopeman. It's always great to be back in your hometown. You miss it when you're not there. As far as you're concerned, it's the best place in the world.

Like Nick and Gizzard I moved to the city to find work. But in many ways we never left our hometowns. We carry them in our minds. You can take the man out of Langholm or Hopeman . . . You almost feel sorry for someone not brought up where you were raised. But if they're lucky enough, they'll feel the same way about their hometown.

'It's still the best Common Riding. In one of them – Musselburgh or Melrose – they dress up as Roman Centurions. What the hell is that? They make things up. This is real. We're marking our ancestors. It's the Border Reivers spirit. Self-sufficient, fiercely proud.

'This field, it's the Parthenon, without the bloody roof. You can go around the world and see everything else, but nothing beats this place. That's why it tugs on the heartstrings. That's why the songs exist.

'Langholmite first. Borderer second. Scotsman third. We are kinda blessed. Out of the world and into Langholm. It is different. "Better felt than telt." You could write a million words and still never express what it feels like. It's difficult to explain to Londoners.'

We ended up back on the barley bannock again. Nick would give it one more twirl tonight. 'Nick spins the bannock wi a lot o' gallus,' agreed Gizzard. 'That fish'll be stinking now . . .'

'One year, the barley bannock disappeared, mind,' said Nick to Gizzard. 'It ended up in a car. Some buggers fae Hawick nicked it. We tracked them doon and owt the sun roof it went. That was it. "Yer banned." They were ostracised.'

'There's an auld rivalry,' said Gizzard, 'but fowk fae Hawick and Langholm are pally.'

He nodded and indicated a group of giant men from Hawick, enjoying their drinks.

The drink was taking its toll in the sense that some of us had to risk the portaloos, which had been re-branded Borderloos. 'It's a dicey proposition.' said Nick. Gizzard was bravest and went first. 'He's a good crack, Gizzard,' said Nick. 'There's nae lull.'

I was either feeling a bit tired or a bit drunk or a bit both. 'When ye're feeling a wee bit jiggedy, hae a lie doon,' offered Nick and I thanked him for his advice.

He gave me a couple of useful pointers on how to sound like you're from Langholm during the Common Riding. 'Every year, fowk say "it's the best yin yet". Every year.' Nick re-commended that for the rest of the day I say 'auld style' a lot, peppering my conversation with this timeless Langholm phrase. 'If ye say "auld style", ye can get away wi' a lot.'

Nick had to go and freshen up for the evening procession. 'I've got tae get the bloody rosette and tie on again. Back tae the mither's for a shower.'

Gizzard kindly invited me back to his for supper. I met his mum and dad and was offered sandwiches, which I wolfed down. 'We dinna make tea on a day like this,' explained Gizzard's mum. 'There's not enough time.' I was delighted with the sandwiches and demolished a few more. I had to bulk myself up for a long night on the Tommy Todds. 'This is the Common Riding fare, these sandwiches,' smiled Gizzard.

The telly was on in the corner, the news reminding me that there was a world outside Langholm. The SNP had just taken Glasgow East from Labour in the by-election.

Gizzard wanted to show me some of Hugh McDiarmid's poetry. McDiarmid, one of Scotland's greatest poets, is a Langholm man. McDiarmid's most famous work is his epic poem *A Drunk Man Looks At The Thistle*, in which the eponymous drunk man ends up lying on a hillside in the moonlight staring at a thistle. A thistle maybe not quite as big as the one I'd been stunned by earlier in the day. The drunk man sees the prickly but beautiful thistle as encapsulating the divided Scottish self. He thinks about his national flower and about the fate of Scotland as a nation. He thinks about his own worries and fears.

But Gizzard was keen on highlighting some of McDiarmid's lesser-known poems – at least lesser-known outside Langholm – poems like 'A Langholm Exile Dreams of Home'. 'He wrote it on a ship in the China Straits, during the war. He's thinking he can't get back. The Common Riding still went on during the war.' Gizzard fondly recited the final phrase. 'The trap is set, the flag is furled, for a' Langholm across the world.' He then brought me to another of McDiarmid's poems, 'Drums in the Walligate'. It is all about the Common Riding, a day like today.

> *Drums in the Walligate, pipes in the air,*
> *Come and hear the cryin' o' the Fair,*
> *A' as it used to be when I was a loon,*
> *On Common Ridin day in the Muckle Toon*
>
> *The Bearer twirls the Bannock and Saut-Herrin',*
> *The Croon o' Roses through the lift is fairin',*
> *The aucht-fit thistle wallops on hit,*
> *In heather besoms a' the hills gang by.*

Full of poetry and sandwiches, we went back to the Castle-holm where there was open-air dancing under a clear blue sky. It was Langholm's big day and the best day of the summer. I was getting bothered by midgies but I could live with it. I was having such a good time. After some dancing – and drinking – it was time to leave the field and get back to the Market Cross. The final procession was led by the Cornet and the whole town started walking, with the band playing 'Auld Lang Syne'. And then the walk turned into the polka. Thousands of people, for hundreds of yards, dancing the polka in the streets. I'd never danced the polka, not in the street, not anywhere, but Nick's mum kept me right. It was polka madness in both directions, ahead of us and behind us, a potential world record for public polka dancing. The traffic lights were at red, but it made no difference. No car was getting through this. 'Are you foo?' someone asked me. Foo meant drunk. I wasn't drunk; I was just a bad dancer. One-two-three hop . . . This was fun. 'Hawick, Langholm, there's nothing between them. They're baith fucking magic,' shouted a polka-dancing man, from either Hawick or Langholm.

The polka continued all the way to the Market Square for the closing ceremony. Everyone was still holding hands. You could feel a special energy. The Cornet rode through the crowd. The dignitaries were waiting. I spotted Nick with the barley bannock. I scratched my head at the giant thistle. The Cornet returned the Burgh flag. No words were said during the handover. Then the officiating magistrate spoke. He praised the Cornet and the weather. 'Cornet Richardson, what can we say? What an absolutely marvellous day. The weather has been brilliant and our Cornet has been supported by record crowds. It's the best yin yet.' I smiled at that, remembering what Nick had said. It was definitely my best yin yet.

'The scenes on the Kirk Wynd this morning had to be seen to be believed,' continued the speaker. 'I think we can say the future of the Common Riding is in safe hands, but there is no sight more moving on a night like this than that of the Cornet and his supporters rounding the corner into the High Street on their return from the Castleholm. It's such a fine spectacle. A Common Riding is judged by the weather and judged by its Cornet. Today the weather has been perfect and the Cornet has been absolutely outstanding. Cornet Richardson, this morning I entrusted to you the flag of the Burgh of Langholm. I charged you to carry it aloft with honour and dignity and asked you to return it tonight unstained and unsullied. Simon, we have not been disappointed. You have raised the bar and set the standard for future Cornets to follow. You have been a credit to yourself and your family and a credit to the Langholm Common Riding. Congratulations on a job well done. What a day!'

Then it was the Cornet's turn. He kept it short and sweet. He thanked his family and friends and the people of Langholm. He received three cheers – and an extra one.

What can I say about Langholm Common Riding? Well, they say it's better felt than telt, but I hope I've given a flavour of it. I've certainly developed a taste for it. And the Tommy Todds. No wonder Nick goes back every year. I'll have to join him again.

About a Hat

– Hat and Ribbon Race, Inverkeithing –

As invitations go, it was unturndownable: 'The Royal Burgh of Inverkeithing has the pleasure of inviting Mr Gary Sutherland to the Hat and Ribbon Race, Friday 1st August. Assemble at the Town House, Inverkeithing, 6.30pm.' I was more than willing to assemble myself for the Hat and Ribbon Race. I wouldn't have missed it for the world. I wasn't doing anything else, but I wouldn't have missed it for the world. I was already there. Well, I was on my way.

My train was on time and my mind was ticking overtime. I'd never encountered a Hat and Ribbon Race before. And this was *the* Hat and Ribbon Race. What did it involve? Well, a hat surely, and a ribbon or ribbons. But what was the role of the hat in the race? Did all the runners wear hats? Who said it was a running race? Maybe it was a bike race – cyclists in bowler hats and with ribbons in their hair. I'd decided they were bowler hats. There's no way they were cowboy hats. That would be ridiculous.

I crossed that Forth Bridge when I came to it – always a stupendous thrill – and shortly afterwards arrived in Inverkeithing. I walked up the hill to the town centre to discover that the Hat and Ribbon Race wasn't the only show in town. A fairground had taken over the High Street. It was a riot of loud bleeps and flashing lights. I looked up at the big wheel and backed off from some giant contraption called The Limbo Dancer with its giant colourful cartoonish pictures of girls in bikinis and boys in shorts, all tanned and having a good time, much like the kids of Inverkeithing – though they weren't tanned and were mostly wearing coats because they live in Scotland, not California. Mind you, if they wanted tans they could acquire them at Sunshine On Fife, the tanning salon across the road. Every High Street has one, although they're not always called Sunshine On Fife. Sometimes they're called Sunshine On Clackmannanshire instead.

The *o'dour de hot dogs* from the fairground fast food stall (Posh Nosh) didn't tempt me. I had a look in the bookies' window, which had the odds for the first weekend of the Scottish football season. Nothing on the Hat and Ribbon Race. I saw a poster for the Hat and Ribbon Race on a shop door. It said that runners (so it wasn't a bike race) 'have to be residents of Inverkeithing and must be of amateur status'. That ruled out professional Hat and Ribbon runners then.

I found the Hat and Ribbon pub. I was meeting Phil there before the race. Phil lives in this neck of Fife and I'd been looking forward to catching up with him. He's a smashing bloke, Phil. He's married to my mam's cousin Annette. They have a son, Paul, and daughter, Julie. When Stewart and I were children, we once stayed with our cousins Paul and Julie during the summer holidays. My brother and I totally looked up to Paul and Julie, not just because they were taller. They were cool. They were teenagers. Paul had Jean Michel Jarre records and Julie played Yahtzee with us. We'd never heard of Jean Michel Jarre records or played Yahtzee before. Stewart and I were more Shakin' Stevens and Kerplunk.

Over a pint in the Hat and Ribbon, Phil filled me in on Paul's latest adventures as a pilot. Paul was still cool. I told Phil why I was in Inverkeithing on this night and described some of my festival travels . . . Orkney, Shetland, how I'd gone to The Clavie for the first time in my life, even though I'd grown up two miles from Burghead. Phil said he'd heard of the Hat and Ribbon

Race but had never been. He wasn't going tonight either. He and Annette had been invited to friends' for dinner, which was fair enough. I promised Phil I'd report back to him on the Hat and Ribbon Race and let him know whether it would be worth attending next year.

We left the pub, only to be faced by a bouncy castle on the doorstep. It had been inflated while we were having a beer. We walked round the bouncy castle and crossed the road. Phil pointed out a building that had a special history attached to it. Annette had worked there when it was a hair salon. Phil was in the navy. His ship had docked and he walked into the hair salon in his navy uniform and asked Annette to marry him. Everyone has these places of huge significance to them and this was one of Phil's. I enjoyed listening to him reminisce at the scene of his proposal all those years ago.

But Phil had to go now and I had a Hat and Ribbon Race to attend. It was nice seeing Phil in normal circumstances. Too often you only see relatives at weddings and funerals, which means you don't see them that often. The last time I had seen Phil was at my dad's funeral. The pair of them got on great. They both loved golf and liked a laugh.

Already a crowd had gathered outside the Town House and the pipe band was warming up. The wonderful waft from the chip shop on the corner was making me hungry. The dignitaries emerged from the Town House, descending the stone steps. One of the dignitaries was wearing what looked to be an extremely large purse round her neck. She must be the provost. Scotland doesn't have mayors.

Then I saw him: a distinguished-looking gentleman in a snazzy red coat. But the red coat wasn't what caught my eye. It was the spear he was carrying. On the tip of the spear was a black top hat covered with ribbons. He was the Hat and Ribbon Man! Either that or he was pretty eccentric.

And he was off, marching down the middle of the road, all of us following him and the pipe band playing 'Scotland the Brave'. He was the Pied Piper of Inverkeithing, which I guess made the rest of us rats. No, he was the Hat and Ribbon Man. We followed him past the big wheel and The Limbo Dancer as the bagpipes and the Waltzers fought for sonic supremacy. It was a beautiful evening for a Hat and Ribbon Race. Every festival that I'd been to of late had been blessed with exceptional weather. I just needed to live in a Scotland of festivals and I'd never be rained on. Mind you, Whuppity Scoorie was dreich.

I suddenly noticed that my enthusiasm for the Hat and Ribbon Race was so great that I was threatening to overtake the Hat and Ribbon Man. I was in danger of stealing his thunder. I quickly stepped back in line so as to be on the safe side and not cause any offence, especially to a man with a spear. Eventually the procession came to a halt and the band stopped. The Hat and Ribbon Man had led us to the starting line of the Hat and Ribbon Race. He put down his spear and chatted to someone.

A woman with a clipboard was talking to the woman with the giant purse round her neck. My guess was that the woman with the clipboard was the Hat and Ribbon Race adjudicator. She looked very much in charge. There was an air of expectancy in Inverkeithing. I didn't know what to expect. 'One-two . . . check one-two . . . can you hear me?' said a man with a microphone. We could hear him loud and clear.

'Ladies and gentlemen, can you hear me okay? Welcome to the Llamas Race.'

Llamas Race? I thought it was a Hat and Ribbon Race. Had I come to the wrong race? No, I couldn't have, because the Hat and Ribbon Man was here. Llamas Race? Where were all the llamas?

'So we're just going to get off and get started . . . just in case the rain comes along.' There wasn't a cloud in the sky. It was all sun. But Scots can't just enjoy the sunshine. We have to worry that the rain will be along in a minute to ruin our day. Especially when there is the success of an outdoor event at stake. Yet even when there's no event on, when it's simply really nice weather, we struggle to cope with it. We'd rather fear the arrival of big black clouds.

'Oh, it's a bonnie day, isn't it?'

'Aye, but it's forecast rain for the morn.'

In the meantime it was dry.

'First up, the Junior Lammas Race, for girls eight years and under.'

There were no llamas at all. No long-necked woolly mammals from the camel family. He had in fact been saying 'Lammas'. The reality is – and I've never been much good with reality – that the Hat and Ribbon Race is an integral part of the Lammas Fair. Inverkeithing, one of Scotland's oldest royal burghs, once held weekly markets and celebrated five annual fairs – one of which, the Lammas Fair, was revived and is recreated every August. Lammas was the Celtic festival of autumn, whereas llamas are from South America.

'Make your way to the line please.' A woman stood a hundred yards down the road acting as a human bollard. The girls had to run round her and back to the finish line. Shortly before the start, a dad pulled his son from the race. He was under eight for sure, but he wasn't a girl. A beat of the pipe band drum signalled the start of the race. The girls set off, circling the human bollard and hurrying towards the finish line with the crowd cheering and applauding. The woman with the clipboard noted the names of the winner and the runner-up. Next it was the boys' turn, with a staggered start. The announcer took the smaller boys down the road a bit so they could have a head-start and a ghost of a chance against the bigger boys. There was a healthy turnout for this race and lots of shouting from the boys' mums.

My brother and I used to race each other in the street outside our house when we were boys, especially when the Olympics or some other major athletics event was on the telly. Just as when Wimbledon was on, our back patio became Centre Court. At least when rain interrupted play we didn't have Cliff Richard singing out the kitchen window. For our athletics meet, the 100m (we didn't take strict measurements) was a straightforward sprint, first past the lamp post the winner. The 200m involved us running round the corner and hopefully not into a car. Obviously, whichever of us was on the inside lane nearest the kerb had to begin a little further back for fairness' sake. And the 1500m meant us running round the block. We talked about running the marathon, but really it was a non-starter. It would have meant us having to run through The Broch, and no Olympic medal was worth that.

At the Lammas Races, we had reached the main event, the boys' over-15 race – the Hat and Ribbon Race. There was a rush to enter and one boy was thrust into the line-up by his mates. He looked about as ready as a young man would ever be for the Hat and Ribbon Race, with a can of lager in his back pocket. To get himself in the right frame of mind – 'in the zone' I think they call it – he lit a cigarette. He wasn't so much competing in the Hat and Ribbon Race as the Fag and Lager Race.

'I'll go for a pee first, then I'll do it,' Fag and Lager boy said to his girlfriend. But there was no time. The Hat and Ribbon Race was imminent. I'd wager that when he'd woken up this morning he'd had no intention of running the Hat and Ribbon Race. He'd been cajoled into it by his mates, his judgement clouded by beer and bravado. 'Sure, I'll run the Hat and Ribbon Race, I'll show them.' It would also impress the girlfriend.

'This is the Hat and Ribbon Race. The race must be run in everyday clothes.' Can of lager in back pocket was optional. Our hooched-up hero was bursting for the toilet. That he could not stand still had little to do with nervous excitement. 'I'll maybe have a pee along the way.' His girlfriend lit his fag again for him.

I remembered my final-year sports day at Lossie High. I hadn't been drinking or smoking but I did run the second leg of the relay. We were trailing the other teams when I took the baton and I fully expected to lose more ground. But, instead, the strangest thing happened. I proceeded to overtake all of my rivals on the bend, showing them a clean pair of heels I had, until this point in my life, kept hidden. It surprised the hell out of me. I didn't know I could run like that. My brother hadn't known I could run like that. He was watching my greatest sporting moment unfold, with his friends. 'Gee! Who's that?' one of them exclaimed as their eyes tried to adjust to the blurred figure eating up the track on the outside lane. 'That's my brother,' whispered Stewart, all admiration and disbelief. I've never run like that since. It was my finest hour on the field. I pretty much hung up my running shoes after that.

I really wanted to run the Hat and Ribbon Race and roll back the years, but I wasn't from Inverkeithing. Meanwhile Lager Boy had another problem besides his loaded bladder. One of his shoelaces was undone. Instead of dealing with the matter by bending down and tying his shoelace, he took off the shoe, and the other one. He was doing a Zola Budd, except in socks. 'What a beamer,' laughed his girlfriend. I hadn't heard 'beamer' in years and vowed to get using it again whenever embarrassing situations cropped up.

The Hat and Ribbon Race runners tore down the road and out of sight. They were no doubt heading for the Forth Bridge. Lager Boy, perhaps surprisingly, had kept with the early pace. We awaited their return. After a while, two of the runners appeared on the horizon. One of them had a definite lead. He held onto it and stormed over the line to victory. The Hat and

Ribbon Race was his. Fittingly his T-shirt bore the legend 'I have the body of a God'. He was a true Olympian.

More runners came home until there was only one left out there. And guess who that was? Lager Boy. 'No sign of him,' said the girlfriend. 'He's maybe collapsed.' 'He'll be too embarrassed to come back,' said another friend of Lager Boy. 'That's what he gets for smoking,' said the girlfriend. 'He told me he'd do it, and I said "no ye winna".'

The announcer gave the concerned crowd an update on Lager Boy. 'He's okay. I've just been reliably informed he's decided to walk back.' Time passed and still no sign of him. Most people had gone home. Then, there he was, the slow walk of a tired man. He was within staggering distance. He was staggering. Lager Boy's girlfriend went over and gave him a hug and his shoes. He'd left in white socks and come back in black socks. Lager boy explained to his girl the delay in his heroic return. 'I ran doon the bottom and then I went for a pee.' Gasping for breath, he pulled out another cigarette.

The presentation for the Hat and Ribbon Race took place, the winner receiving a cracking trophy from the Hat and Ribbon Man. A little boy told Lager Boy he should have got a medal – a 'not-coming-back medal'. The pipers played 'Scotland the Brave' and then it was high time for the Hat and Ribbon Race Reception – to which I'd been invited!

I entered the hall and joined the queue at the bar. While I waited on a pint, the woman with the clipboard came up to me. 'Are you Gary?' I was. She was Shirley. She had sent me my invitation in the post, after I'd called up about the Hat and Ribbon Race to check when it was on. I wondered how she knew it was me. Then I thought she probably knew everyone else in the room and, aside from that, I was the only one in the hall wearing a backpack and looking like I'd just arrived in Inverkeithing while giving off the general air that I didn't know quite where I was or what I was supposed to be doing. (This is actually my default air.)

Shirley said to come and find her after I'd got my pint. I found her sitting comfortably at the top table with the Hat and Ribbon Man, the lady with the big purse round her neck and a couple of other important-looking people. Shirley gestured to the empty seat next to her. It was for me. Not only had I received an invite to the Hat and Ribbon Race, I'd been granted a seat at the top table, since I was researching a book about Scottish festivals. I wasn't prepared for this level of welcome. I hoped I didn't have to make a speech or anything. I sat down sheepishly and smiled apologetically at the many faces in the hall. Surely they were all wondering 'Who the Hell is he, who let him in?' I took a self-conscious sip of my pint and stared at my feet for a bit. A man further down the top table got up and welcomed everyone before handing over to Shirley.

'I'd like to introduce the top table,' she began. She introduced the woman with the big purse round her neck who turned out to be the Provost of Fife. She was very nice and I said hello. Shirley introduced the Hat and Ribbon Man, who needed no introduction but she gave him a really good one. And then she turned to me. 'This is Mr Gary Sutherland. He's researching and writing a book about Scottish customs and festivals and this is his first Hat and Ribbon Race.' I nodded wisely, trying to fool the audience into thinking I was a man of towering intellect. As long as I didn't have to stand up and open my mouth. I wouldn't have been able to. My mouth was dry and my legs were cement. I sought solace in my pint. It was tough being a guest of honour, what with people staring at you. It wouldn't have been so bad if I'd dressed better for the occasion. I looked like a tramp.

The Provost of Fife made a warm toast to the Hat and Ribbon Race and thanked us all for coming out to watch it. She pointed out the considerable effort – from the likes of Shirley – that went into organising the Hat and Ribbon Race and thought that the children had run well. She'd thoroughly enjoyed the occasion and on such a fine summer's evening, too. She'd been very impressed. She then sat down without ordering me to leave the top table. For now, I was safe. Soon I got up from the top table anyway, to raid the buffet table. I returned to my throne with a paper plateful of sausage rolls and egg sandwiches. I was starting to enjoy myself.

'We've done not badly over the years,' said Shirley, about the Hat and Ribbon Race. 'The actual race, I don't know when it started. But it goes back a few hundred years. It was for the shepherd boys at the market. Flocks of sheep would be sold and the boys would race. We've got documents from 1740 and it's mentioned. The prize for the winner was a top hat and there were ribbons for his girlfriend.'

Today's racing recalled the town's past but without Shirley there probably wouldn't still be a Hat and Ribbon Race and the kids would have had a less exciting evening in Inverkeithing.

'They have to be from Inverkeithing,' said Shirley, 'but we've scrapped the entry form to encourage people to take part. They just turn up and run.'

I couldn't have imagined Lager Boy filling in an entry form.

Shirley introduced me to the Hat and Ribbon Man. His name was Bill. A former policeman, Bill had been performing his Hat and Ribbon duties since 1982. 'I've enjoyed every moment, trying to keep this going,' he smiled. 'If it wasn't for people like Shirley, this would go downhill. Once something is finished, it's very difficult to get it reinstated.'

Bill's son arrived at the top table to collect him. I asked if he minded taking a picture of me and his dad. 'Don't worry, I've taken plenty of pictures,' he laughed, accustomed to his dad being in demand as the Hat and Ribbon Man with his cere-monial coat and decorated spear. I had my picture taken with the

Hat and Ribbon Man in the front lawn and I thanked them. It was time for me to go, too. I thanked Shirley, said goodbye and began my walk to the train station.

The fairground rides were flashing and bleeping and different music was pounding and clashing. I fancied a beer for the train journey back to Glasgow and popped into a shop and plucked my choice off the shelf. The girl at the till eyed me with suspicion. She asked if I was over 25. 'You're joking?' I blurted out, taken aback. Now I saw she was wearing a badge with a big 25 on it. It was this shop's policy that you had to be over 25, rather than the usual 18, to buy alcohol. But even still, I was ten years in the clear. The girl gave me a stern look. She wasn't joking and she didn't appreciate my making light of the situation. She didn't trust me. She asked again.

'Are you over twenty-five?'

'I'm thirty-four!'

'You don't look thirty-four.'

'November 1972. I'm thirty-four'

What was I saying? I wasn't 34. I was 35. Why did I say I was 34? I'd shaved a year off my age and, on top of that, 34 didn't tally with November 1972. What had caused this? Nerves? Vanity? I'd cocked up a question about how old I was. If the girl found the discrepancy in my ill-fitting tale, there was no comeback for me. I was behaving like a liar. A 35-year-old liar. My defence was flawed. It didn't add up. My number was up and I wasn't getting any beer. I may as well have said I was 27 or something, then she might have been more inclined to believe me. I wouldn't have seemed so ridiculous to her. I would still have been lying, but it wouldn't have sounded so boastful.

Now the girl's colleague had taken an interest in me. She was equally skeptical and cross-examined me with her arms folded. 'You don't look thirty-four.' Here we go again. Quite frankly, I was tempted to put the beer back on the shelf. But then they'd have won and I'd have been under 25, in their minds at least. I was not leaving this shop without my beer. I was 35, God dammit. It was my beer, I tell you.

'I'm thirty-four,' I said calmly, sticking to my guns and lying through my teeth. 'You look awful young for thirty-four.' 'Thanks very much.' She didn't like that. Now I was being sarcastic. I stood there defiant, inviting their scorn. Eventually they grudgingly agreed to a transaction. They didn't really believe me, but they wanted rid of me. I thanked them (again managing to sound saracastic) and left the shop before they changed their minds. I had my beer and the youthful face of an under-25-year-old.

I had to call someone, to tell them I'd regained my youth. I called Brian. Not The Manny Willox, but another Brian. I have lots of friends called Brian. One of my ex-girlfriends was called Brian. She was a girl too.

Brian, the Brian I'd just phoned, offered to make me some fake ID so I wouldn't have the problem again. I very much doubted I would have the problem again. Brian then suggested I keep going back to Inverkeithing as I grow older, and try to buy beer, in an effort to defy the ageing process. I told Brian he was being ridiculous. That's the other thing about the Brians I know. They're all ridiculous. I started telling Brian about the Hat and Ribbon Race. 'There was this man, right? And he had a hat . . .'

What I really wanted to do was to turn back the clock and find my clean pair of heels again. Next time I was in Hopeman, I was going to challenge my brother to a race round the block.

The Itchy and Scratchy Show

– *The Burry Man, South Queensferry* –

August in Edinburgh. It was August in Glasgow too. But I happened to be in Edinburgh, where the world's biggest arts festival was going on and offering the arts-loving public such delights as 'Fried Eggs Don't Talk Back', 'Men with Bananas', 'Big Jessie's Bag of Drag', 'The Bollocks of Liechtenstein', 'Eco-Friendly Jihad', 'Nicholas Parsons' Happy Hour' and '1000 Years of German Humour'. If you had the appetite – and I didn't – you could feast on 'Pot Noodle: The Musical', 'The Yorkshire Pudding Paradigm' or 'Why We Ate Cliff Richard'. Why *would* you eat Cliff Richard? For those with higher brows, there was plenty of drama in the form of 'Beowulf', 'The Feast of Ants', 'Hello Dali' and 'What's Wrong with Angry?' This was all well and good – and angry – but what I wanted to see was a man with an antelope strapped to his chin. And there was no mention of that in the listings.

The only reason I was in Edinburgh was because I was trying to get to South Queensferry. It was the Burry Man's day in South Queensferry and nothing Edinburgh had to offer could compete with the Burry Man in terms of sheer spectacle. Not even a man with an antelope strapped to his chin. I had only seen pictures of the Burry Man and he was ten times more scary than the Bogey Man. Frankly, the Burry Man was giving me the fear, but I was going to confront my (not unreasonable) fear of this giant man-plant that stalks the streets of South Queensferry once a year on the second Friday of August.

I'd have to wait a bit longer before I got to South Queensferry though. I was stuck at Haymarket station, kicking about the platform, unable to catch my connecting train because there was a puddle in the tunnel. You get a shower of rain in Scotland and everything grinds to a halt. Since it rains most days in Scotland, most days things grind to a halt. You just have to grind your teeth and bare them, while awaiting further announcements, or any kind of an announcement. After a great deal of silence and confusion, it was announced that, due to the puddle in the tunnel, there would be no trains going to South Queensferry. Great. Instead, they were laying on a replacement bus service. Fantastic.

I'd had better days. When the bus eventually turned up, it had seen better days. A dozen of us displaced passengers were herded onto the clapped-out vehicle. Once we were velcroed to our sticky seats, the driver turned round and happily admitted that he didn't know where he was going. He wondered if any of us could help him out with directions. The clueless driver was so brimming with bonhomie that you couldn't possibly be angry at him. So we all forgot about the ridiculousness and rottenness of our situation and pitched in with our suggestions of how to get to such-and-such-a-place. We laughed at our predicament and snorted in the face of inconvenience. What fun we were having on the magic bus. Knowledgeable and helpful souls – already extremely late for work or meetings or wherever they were going – patiently advised the chirpy and whistling driver. When the magic bus reached South Queensferry, I wanted to stay on and remain part of the magical mystery tour. Reluctantly I got off, thanking the driver for dropping me off in South Queens-ferry two hours later than I'd intended to be there. I walked down the street with a spring in my step and a smile on my face.

I could smell the sea even before I glimpsed the Firth of Forth. Directly above my head was the incredible red skeleton of the

Forth Bridge. I looked up in awe as a train hurtled past (not my train then). Down by the waterfront, the bridge – this incredible achievement of Scottish engineering and a national icon – rightly drew the eyes of tourists and the lenses of their cameras. The Forth Bridge is one of the finest sights in Scotland and the charming town of South Queensferry basks in its glory. You can't get much more picturesque than this.

In John Buchan's classic spy thriller, *The 39 Steps*, the hero Richard Hannay, wrongly suspected of murder, is cornered on the Flying Scotsman as it crosses the Forth Bridge. In his desperation, the dashing Hannay pulls the emergency cord and leaps from his berth onto the track. In the film *The 39 Steps*, Alfred Hitchcock had Hannay swinging up into the bridge's girders. This morning, loads of tourists were gawping at the girders. I didn't suppose any of them had encountered the Burry Man yet. If they had, they'd have been leaping into the ice-cold Firth to escape his spiky clutches.

I continued along the cobbled street, hoping to catch my first glimpse of the Burry Man. He was around somewhere. I knew that he began his deranged walk around town at nine o' clock in the morning. It was now after ten. I'd planned to be there at the start but the trains had made sure that I wasn't, even if I had left the house at six in the morning for a journey that should have taken two hours tops. So where was the Burry Man? He wasn't exactly easy to miss. He'd certainly stand out in a crowd, being a ghastly and prickly green giant and all that.

I caught the red reflection of the bridge in the window of a sweetie shop. Apart from the bridge, the window displayed jars of all kinds of toothy delights: Liquorice Saturns, Everton Mints, Berwick Cockles, Hawick Balls, Pontefract Cakes, Toffee Doddles and, my childhood favourite, Peardrops (though I was often torn between Peardrops and Sherbet Strawberries). The yellow bunting that hung above the street was to signify that this was the week of the annual Ferry Fair. You could hardly miss the fairground stretching along the esplanade either.

Water dripped onto the pavement from the freshly watered flower baskets of the Ferry Tap pub. 'Have you seen the Burry Man?' I asked a man. 'What man?' asked the man. The man was a tourist, German by the sounds of him. He didn't know anything about the Burry Man. I cursed not having a picture of the Burry Man to show him. That would have been interesting. He might have jumped into the Firth, or at least have boarded his tour bus. I thanked him anyway and wished him a good day.

Where was he, the human hedge? I heard the intro to Prince's 'Controversy'. I had a text message. It was Brian. Not the Brian from the end of the last chapter, nor The Manny Willox. No, this was The Third Brian. I told you I knew lots of Brians. This Brian lived in Edinburgh. He was planning to join me later on, after he'd finished work. 'How's the Burry Man?' read Brian's message. I texted back saying I hadn't found him yet. Brian thought this was hilarious. Intro to Prince's 'Controversy'. 'Ha ha. Furry boots the Burry Man?' I'd no idea furry boots the Burry Man was. But, in the meantime, I could tell you something about him.

On the second Friday of August, the Burry Man comes out to play (and suffer horribly). The Burry Man is a man – not a normal man, but a man – covered from head to ankle in burrs. Burrs are the seed pods from the burdock plant. They're a bit like thistles. Imagine being covered head to ankle in thistles and you've got the general idea. The scientific name for the burdock plant is *Artimus Bardana*. It translates as 'ooyah bastard'. The burdock plant is a member of the daisy family, but there's nothing so pleasant about this member of the daisy family. Burrs are vicious scratchy things and why you'd want to decorate yourself from top to bottom in them is anyone's guess. I'd need to ask the Burry Man himself – if I could face looking him in the eyes. The fact you can see the Burry Man's eyes is perhaps the most terrifying part. I hoped he wouldn't be too prickly and would suffer my questions, as well as having to be the Burry Man.

In the build-up to the Burry Man's big day, the burrs are foraged from the countryside by the Burry Man and his friends. The burrs are gathered in bags, brought back and left to dry. All beasties are removed. Hundreds of patches are made with the burrs, no adhesive needed. The spike ends of the burrs are like hooks. They have a ferocious grip. The Burry Man is fitted into his patchwork suit of burrs at seven in the morning. His fitters start from the ankles and work up to his face. Great care is taken with sensitive areas, such as the crotch, knees and armpits. It's a two-hour job dressing the Burry Man. He wears clothes underneath the burrs and wears a light balaclava, but the nasty and persistent burrs still have the knack of working their way through to the skin. And apart from that discomfort, it gets very hot in there, when you're burried in burrs.

The Burry Man hits the High Street and soon after that hits the drink. Well, a plant needs watering. With nine terrible hours ahead of him, he needs some kind of coping mechanism, and that coping mechanism is whisky. The Burry Man seeks sustenance through a straw. Throughout the Burry Man's day, he is plied with drink by well-wishers and the Burry Man gladly accepts. He's a formidable whisky-soaked entity, the Burry Man. But where is he?

And what's the point of the Burry Man? Is it about bewildering the tourists, frightening the children and making dogs bark? It's the strangest custom I've come across. The tradition of the Burry Man may be up to 900 years old, though the first recording of him is 1687. It's not a video recording. The origin of the Burry Man is shrouded in burrs. No one is sure how he came about; not even the Burry Man knows. It could have been a Pagan ritual, invoking good fortune. There's the idea of the Burry Man as the village scapegoat, carrying away from the town a year's worth of evil, since he's spiky enough to catch all the bad spirits. Maybe the point of the Burry Man was to ensure a good fishing season. It's said there were once similar figures in other coastal communities like Buckie and Fraserburgh. Perhaps the Burry Man is a symbol of fertility. There are parallels with the Green Man of folklore. He's most definitely green. Or did he emerge from the sea covered in burrs like some crazy plant fish? Or is he a baddie from *Dr Who*? Dr Who would lock himself in his Tardis if confronted by the Burry Man. Is the Burry Man simply the Burgh Man? Sir Walter Scott tried to unearth the truth about the Burry Man but was stumped. Scott drew a blank with the sinister man-plant.

I headed up the hill past the church and heard bells. They weren't coming from the church. A few boys were crossing the road ahead of me and ringing bells and behind them was . . . the Burry Man! What a fright. What a sight. It wasn't surprising he was stopping traffic. Drivers gawped at the Burry Man. A dog stopped and sniffed the Burry Man's boots. The Burry Man posed for some pictures. He was an obliging Burry Man. He then started chatting to a passing friend about what was on the friend's iPod. This was surreal. A car drew up and the driver leaned out the window and asked the Burry Man if he was 'okay for the Hibs the morn?' The Burry Man nodded. He was John Nicol, a 34-year-old Hibs supporter, which may explain his capacity for pain. John had been Burry Man for the past decade and was supported by his dad, John Snr, and his Uncle Alex. Dad poked his fingers in the Burry Man's eyes. Not to be cruel, but to let some air in, to help his son feel more comfortable. There was a tenderness to it.

I considered the Burry Man. He looked menacing but he was more benign than belligerent. His arms were outstretched as he held onto two staves, garlanded with flowers. His arms had to be away from his sides, otherwise they'd stick. The Burry Man wore a crown of roses and sported a Lion Rampant flag-cum-cummerbund round his waist. He was beauty and the beast.

The perambulation of the plant man looked gruelling. I couldn't even begin to imagine the degree of discomfort. It had to be both physically and psychologically demanding. This was masochism of the highest order. And he did this all day? I had to get to the bottom of this and find the man beneath the burrs.

A woman wanted her picture taken with the Burry Man. 'Don't blush,' she joked. 'It's hot,' said the Burry Man's dad. 'Get him into the shade.' The sun was a threat. It could wilt this walking plant. The Burry Man bumped into a group of toddlers out for a walk with their nursery teacher. The children looked stunned. One girl in a buggy was terrified. She burst into tears. 'It's okay,' soothed her teacher, 'he's away.' But that image was burned in that child's mind. How could she forget the Burry Man? He'd be chasing her in her nightmares, the poor thing. A man on a ladder was trimming his hedge. The Burry Man had to steer clear of those shears. There were plenty of words of encouragement for the Burry Man. 'Good on you,' said a fan, 'I hope you have a few bevvies tonight.' 'He's had a few already,' said the Burry Man's dad.

'Hip hip hooray, it's the Burry Man's day!' cried the boys who were ringing their bells and shaking their buckets for donations. A mother asked her little girl if she'd like her photo taken with the Burry Man. The daughter recoiled in horror. She wanted to be as far away from the Burry Man as possible. But the Burry Man was in sore need of a breather. He leaned against a tree. It afforded him some momentary respite and some welcome shade. A woman in her front garden pointed at the tree and said: 'My husband wants to cut it down, but I say leave it for the Burry Man.'

We passed a school. The Burry Man's uncle invited some

pupils to meet the Burry Man. 'C'mon, c'mon, he'll no bite ye.' They weren't convinced and declined the invitation. Further along the road, one boy showed more bravery. He reached out and took a burr from the Burry Man. He held it in his hand, looking pleased with himself. I thought of The Clavie and people taking a piece. Here you could have your memento of the Burry Man, if you had the courage.

It was mid-morning and fairly low key. There weren't many folk following the Burry Man. Any conversation was of the everyday kind. A woman told the Burry Man about her holidays. We then reached a house where a couple came out to offer the Burry Man a dram. 'Good health! How are you?' asked the woman. 'It's pretty warm,' said the Burry Man in a gentle voice. 'You're looking good though, very colourful again,' said the woman, who added that he'd just got a mention on the radio.

Another house and another dram. 'It's coloured water,' explained the man to the Burry Man. It was coloured alright, the colour of whisky with a drop of water in it. I talked to a woman who smiled at the Burry Man and said how much she looked forward to this day. 'I always try and take the day off. When we were children, we were running about at the crack of dawn trying to find him. Your mam would say to you "don't come back till you're hungry", but we didn't even come back when we were hungry. There used to be hundreds of kids following him. We all used to shout "Hip hip hooray it's the Burry Man's day", so everybody would come out of their houses. But nowadays, so many people are working and you don't get that, and people aren't too keen letting their kids wander the streets all day. But it's an age-old tradition and I don't like to let it go past. I don't think this will die out. I just hope that when John's had enough that somebody can take it on from him. He's done well. It's a big commitment, but it's not easy. Especially when it's hot like this, 'cause he's got so many layers on. He does well.'

The Burry Man was getting stuck into an Islay malt. 'Personally yes,' he said when asked if the day before would have been a better day for it, given that the weather was cooler and the sun wasn't as strong as it was now. There was a police car behind us. They'd have some job getting handcuffs on the Burry Man. But it turned out they weren't after him.

I learned from the Burry Man about the hazards of the job, like the several wasp stings he took last year. 'It was like getting a nail in the forehead. I didn't really notice till the next day. The burrs get through and scratch you. It can be pretty painful and it can start off a chain reaction. I was explaining to a friend about when you have an itch on your shoulder or your foot, you're aware of it. If you challenge yourself – "I'm not going to bother itching it" it gets more and more unbearable. I've got hundreds of bits and pieces that need attention and you kind of get to the point it becomes almost like a drone, a sensation . . . and that's where the whisky really helps. It knocks you out a bit. It's crazy.

'If it's raining, this weighs a ton. The burrs take the water like a sponge. Then, when it's warm, not too warm, it's comfortable. The burrs start to kind of crackle. You really hear them crackling. Every year there are different characteristics. It's not a case of once you've done it, that's what it's like. It's the physicality that's difficult.'

Does it not get claustrophobic in there?

'I am actually claustrophobic. I just try not to think about it.'

How could he not think about it? It's all I was thinking about. But that's one of a million reasons why I'm not the Burry Man.

It was after midday and time for the Burry Man's first toilet break. He does his best to keep it in – 'it's more a psychological thing; in the afternoon it gets really awkward' – but sometimes the call of nature is too strong and his dad and uncle have to cut him free carefully with a pair of scissors so he can have a leak wherever he can. Then they patch him up again. The Burry Man dealt with his pressing need and soon after was tackling another whisky. How many whiskies had he had? 'Nine so far.'

'There's the straw,' said a woman, guiding it towards his mouth. 'I can't see it.' 'It's there. Other way.' 'No, you're putting it up his nose,' said his uncle. She finally got there and laughed. 'That's it.' 'Thank you,' said the Burry Man. 'Somebody tried to put it in his eye earlier on,' said his dad. Whisky polished off, the Burry Man was off on his travels again. 'Hip hip hooray, it's the Burry Man's day.'

I met the Burry Man's friends George and Stevie. They'd be escorting the Burry Man next year. This was John Snr's and Alex's final year as chaperones of the Burry Man. They'd be retiring from duty after today. 'I'm getting the practice in,' said George, raising the glass of whisky in his hand. 'When John's dad and uncle retire, me and Stevie will take it over. Dressed up in tartan trews . . . plenty whiskies on the day . . . it's not pub measures either. You don't know what you're drinking. You'll see his dad and uncle by the end of it. They're worse than John because he gets to sweat it all out. But the pair of them . . .'

Stevie, who'd be taking one of the Burry Man's arms for the first time next year, said, 'That won't be me taking him to the toilet though.'

I asked George what he thought of John being the Burry Man. 'It's a typical John thing to do. None of our other friends would have done it. If anyone was going to be the Burry Man, it's him. He's the personality to do it. John is quite natural.

'You slap the burrs and patches on him and fill in the gaps. Once he gets the mask on that's him for the day. He'll not joke in the morning. He's serious. We were out for a couple of pints last night and he said he just wakes up in the morning and that's it. He's in the zone. Rather him than me. I can't do it; I'm Glasgow anyway. You've got to be born here. You have to be from South Queensferry and your dad has to be from South Queensferry. I don't know if that's something that'll continue when John finishes. There's a fairly small pool of people. John can keep going for as long as he wants to and feels he can continue.

'No one can really say what the Burry Man is about or why we do it, but I suppose it's something that should carry on. It's a form of torture though really, isn't it? Nine till six. It must have been for the bad ones in the past. Thirty days in the jail, or you're the Burry Man. I'll take the jail. The relief when he gets his boots off and stuff, it's palpable. It's funny. There's only one year he struggled and that was with the heat. The burrs get to everything. Now he'll be scratched and cut and sore. It's horrible.'

There was a stop for lunch at the Burry Man's house, with a crowd of family and friends in a marquee in the back garden. The Burry Man was benefiting the most from the marquee. It was a chance to escape the sun. It was a seriously warm day. Water was poured over the Burry Man's shoulders, to cool him down, like he was a racehorse. A Hibs shirt hung from an upstairs window. BURRY MAN it said on the back. Lunch over, the Burry Man braved the heat again and the lonely trudge resumed. He had company, but only he was inside that suit.

A woman put a pound coin in a donation bucket. She'd lived in South Queensferry forty years but this was the first time she'd seen the Burry Man. Another woman slowed down in her car and rolled down the window. 'Excuse me, what's this?' It was a perfectly reasonable question. I did my best to explain.

The Burry Man leaned against a wall for comfort. An old lady walked up to him and asked how he was doing. She wanted one of his burrs and he gave her permission to take one. A few kids got the same idea and soon they were all piling in for their jagged souvenirs. It was hard being the Burry Man, but John wore it well. He had infinite patience and was totally happy talking to people when he was going through agony. Talking may have taken his mind off it. The Burry Man was led into a pub and the daytime drinkers almost choked on their pints. One of the Burry Man boys rang his bell for cash. 'Is that last orders?' asked a punter. The opening ceremony of the Olympic Games was on the telly, the athletes of all the countries proudly waving as they paraded round the track. Bahrain . . . Cuba . . . The Burry Man left the pub and soldiered on. 'Bye Burry Man,' shouted a boy in the street. John Snr soon had his fingers in his son's eyes again, trying to address at least some of his son's discomfort, another display of care from a dad on gardening duty.

We crossed a busy road at traffic lights. The green man was apt. It was time to visit Tesco and shock the shoppers. 'Hip hip hooray, it's the Burry Man's day.' People leaving the supermarket almost dropped their bags in fright. The Burry Man rested against a bunch of shopping trolleys. While he made himself semi-comfortable, the supermarket staff brought him a drink. This time it was a soft drink.

'This is a form of suffering,' exclaimed an incredulous American tourist. 'Someone has to do it,' deadpanned the Burry Man, before adding: 'I'm trying to make things nice.' I thought this was the whisky talking, but then I reconsidered and decided that the Burry Man really meant it. He was trying to make things nice. He looked in a bad way but he was full of goodwill. He was still ever so slightly sozzled in the sizzling heat.

The Burry Man spoke softly as he explained to the American why he was the Burry Man. 'What's important to me is the tradition, that it happens every year and we want to make sure that when I'm not there to do it there'll be someone else there to do it, a continuation of it—'

Someone interrupted the Burry Man. They wanted his autograph. 'Do you want me to sign it "Burry Man"?' asked the Burry Man. Somehow he was capable of scribbling a signature. 'It's cool that people come out,' he continued. 'That's an amazing thing. It's part of the effort.'

His enthusiasm was effortless. You felt good being around the Burry Man. His positivity rubbed off on you. Being in his company for a moment gave people a warm glow. You could see it in their faces. Never judge a Burry Man by his burrs. He was all grace under pressure, oozing positivity and whisky through his pores.

It was after three o' clock – three hours still to go – and the decision was taken by the Burry Man's handlers to slow down a bit. The Burry Man was feeling a little shaky. He wobbled on the pavement and his dad and uncle propped him up against a wall, offering him words of comfort. There was a constant danger of overheating with the sun beating down on the Burry Man. More water was poured on the Burry Man's shoulders. He was in some pain. You felt for him. But you didn't know how he felt.

A second supermarket and another impromptu photo-shoot. Bystanders made their demands and the Burry Man obliged. He had found another set of shopping trolleys to lean on, and he was in the shade. What a blessed relief. A girl posed with the Burry Man. He had plenty of female admirers. Some of them were wearing burrs in their hair. The Burry Man was their hero.

'For another wee dram?' someone asked him. 'Aye, cool.' When he wasn't sucking on the straw, the Burry Man pondered his role in society. 'No one's sure what it's about. The most important thing for me is that it carries on and at the moment I'm the one that's doing it. Ten years I've done it. That's ten years less to worry about.'

He got to the end of his whisky and announced: 'I don't really like whisky, but it serves a purpose. When I'm hot it gets comfortable – in a funny sort of way. You just sort of become activated. It's weird.' What's weird is being claustrophobic and not liking whisky and becoming the Burry Man and drinking whisky all day. He was either a marvel or a maniac.

A group of cool kids invited the Burry Man to a party in

Edinburgh. 'You'll be the star of everything, the hero of the evening.' The Burry Man had to pass. 'Aww,' sighed a girl. If you want popularity with the girls, dress up as the Burry Man. They'll hug you and kiss you and paw you – despite the threat of cuts – and invite you to parties. A local lady who knew the Burry Man approached and said, 'It's lovely to see you . . . sort of.'

The Burry Man was on the home straight now. Rain had been forecast for some point during the day, but it hadn't happened. 'I think we're doing okay,' said John Snr. 'When you're finished,' said the Burry Man, 'you're just, like, "get me oot o this".' He reckoned he'd walked twelve miles, all told. We stopped in a beer garden with a great view of the Forth Road Bridge. There was more whisky and more friends willing him on. 'C'mon, John boy.' They had come to support him on the final leg of his journey along the High Street.

There was a growing sense of jubilation. The Burry Man seemed to have regained some of his strength in the past half-hour. He was becoming more agile, as if he'd cast off those burrs already and was a free man again. Down the High Street he traipsed, his dad and uncle the faithful sentinels. Along the esplanade, past the fairground (a great spot for scaring kids), towards the Forth Bridge. 'Are you a bit drunk?' someone asked the Burry Man. 'You only get drunk when you fall,' said the Burry Man's dad.

What a combination: the Burry Man and the Forth Bridge. And the blissful weather. A tourist took a snap from a safe distance. 'His name's John,' shouted John Snr. They turned back from the bridge and were piped along the road to their final destination, where they'd originally set out from nine hours ago. The Staghead.

Brian had joined me just in time and was getting his first look at the Burry Man. 'It must be the nearest you can get to wearing an internal balaclava,' said Brian. Now my cousins were here too.

Phil and Annette, and Paul and his wife, Philippa, and their children. They'd all popped over the bridge to say hello and see some of the Burry Man action. They were as bemused as Brian was – as bemused as anyone encountering the Burry Man for the first time.

We were inside the Staghead. John was still inside the burrs. But he was sitting on a chair and was about to be freed. Everyone gathered round to watch. First the head of burrs was removed and raised in the air. It was a dramatic moment. And for the first time I saw the man beneath, except you couldn't see John's face. His head was slumped forward, as if he'd been hypnotised. There was just a mass of matted long hair. Slowly he roused himself. He flicked back his hair and grinned. He looked like he had awoken from the deepest sleep. He was cut from the rest of his suit and sat there in his faded jeans and T-shirt. The man inside had been released. John rose to his feet and lurched forward. He then started pacing about, taking the applause. He had no idea where he was, by the looks of it. He must be steaming. He started taking his socks off. People were patting him on the back. I got a high-five from him. Then he was off to the toilet for the biggest pee of his life, or at least the biggest pee since the last time he was the Burry Man. What a guy.

What a bizarre day. The Burry Man is absurd, but special and certainly unique. It takes someone extraordinary like John Nicol to be the Burry Man. He has an unyielding desire for this ancient custom not to die out. How he does it, I do not know.

Pipe Dreams and Haggis Nightmares

– *Birnam Highland Games, Birnam* –

I was travelling by train to Birnam in Perthshire and almost everyone in my carriage was a bagpiper. Yes, it's Scotland, but this isn't an everyday scene. The pipers were blethering about jigs and reels and 68s and 24s. One blowhard was droning on about the importance of reed maintenance. 'I just play them,' his friend cut in, attempting to head off any further dull chat about pipe cleaning.

I had never been to a Highland Games before. The reason for that is simple: I'm Scottish. Scots don't go to Highland Games. Highland Games are for tourists. Just like Edinburgh, and Pitlochry for some reason. I have to say, though, I was looking forward to some old-fashioned caber tossing. And I was expecting bagpipes. Judging by the company on the train, I wasn't going to be disappointed on that count.

The pipers and I piled off at Birnam and Dunkeld station. (Two villages, one station; the River Tay splits Birnam and Dunkeld.) I'd passed through the station countless times en route to Inverness, but this was the first time I'd ever got off there. The first time I ever heard of Birnam was reading *Macbeth* at school, Birnam Wood moving to Dunsinane being part of the witches' prophecy.

The scenery is quintessentially Perthshire, with impossibly green hills. I strolled down a pleasant country lane and into Birnam, where the residents were taking full advantage of the warm weather, cutting their grass and trimming their hedges. A vintage car cruised past, its driver in no particular hurry. The tearoom across the road looked busy. I imagined their customers were tucking into scones. A girl walked past wearing a badge that said 'This badge belongs to Lionel Richie'. This puzzled me greatly. It wasn't just the badge. The week before I'd been on a train and on the back of the seat in front of me was a sticker. It said 'This seat belongs to Lionel Richie'. Hello? What was Lionel Richie up to? Was he going around Scotland handing out badges to strangers and leaving stickers on trains?

I forgot about Lionel Richie because I suddenly spotted the most Scottish road sign in the whole of Scotland. It pointed in the directions of the following places: Inverness, Crianlarich, Blairgowrie and Coupar Angus. The only destination missing was Auchtermuchty.

I was nearing the entrance gate to the Highland Games. I was surrounded by accents other than my own. I heard Americans and Australians, or else they were Kiwis and Canadians. I could hear French and Spanish being spoken, because I'm a dab hand at those languages. The Frenchman was asking his girlfriend 'où est la piscine?' and the Spanish girl was saying to her mother 'una cerveza, por favor', which didn't make sense, because there wasn't a bar in sight. I felt like the lone Scotsman in their midst, a stranger in my own country. So far, my notion that Highland Games were for tourists wasn't far off the mark. It was pretty much bang on the money.

Men in fluorescent bibs and kilts (the kilts weren't fluorescent) were directing cars towards parking spaces. I paid my admission money at the gate and bought a programme. I opened it to be welcomed a hundred thousand times in several different tongues. *Ceud Mile Failte* (I think that's one of ours), *Bienvenue Cent Milles Fois, Seien Sie Hunderttausendmal Wilkommen, Cien Mil Bienvenidos, Een Honderd Duizend Maal Welkom, Hundra Tusen Vakomsthalsninger*. That last one was clearly made-up.

The Birnam Highland Games is almost a century and a half old. There are more than a hundred Highland Games in Scotland. The Highland Games season is between May and September. The end of August sees the Cowal Gathering in Dunoon, the biggest Highland Games in the world, with competitors and spectators flocking from all over the world. The Highland Games became popular in the early nineteenth century when there was a concerted drive to romanticise Highland culture. Queen Victoria gave the get-togethers a real boost when she attended the Braemar Gathering in 1848. She came second in the hammer throwing.

There were lots of stalls at Birnam Highland Games and I checked them out for typical Scottish produce. I was specifically looking for tablet. There must be tablet, I thought. I found clogs, bush hats and Tibetan shawls – all synonymous with Scotland. You don't walk down Union Street in Aberdeen on a Saturday night without your clogs on. Bush hats are more a Dundonian thing, while sporting a Tibetan shawl is a dead giveaway that you're from Lanarkshire, probably Airdrie. Beyond the clogs, bush hats and Tibetan shawls, there were bum-bags (which should really have been labelled 'fanny packs' for the American market), Loch Ness leather wallets (made from the hide of the monster), tea towels (with pictures of Scottie dogs), and mantelpieces. Who, in their right mind, would go to a Highland Games and come home with a mantelpiece?

When I reached the sweetie stall, I felt that my goal was near. Gobstoppers . . . fudge bars, and – yes – tablet! Hand-made whisky tablet! I bought some as a treat for my teeth. I didn't bother buying a ticket for the SNP tombola though. I wasn't tempted by what Alex Salmond's party had to offer. First prize was a bottle of Lambrusco. Second prize was a bottle of ginger wine – which was probably Lambrusco mixed with Irn-Bru.

The Shot Putters' Bar wasn't open yet. I made a mental note to have my pint of Tartan Special later on. In the meantime, I watched a sprint race. The winner romped home in 9.53 seconds. Surely it was a new world record. That Jamaican runner would be gutted when he found out he'd been overtaken by a man from Hawick at the Birnam Highland Games. Then I learned it was the 90m race – not the 100m. The world record was safe and the world made sense again.

Men in kilts strutted about flogging bottles of whisky from baskets. Some spectators were spectacularly prepared for the Games in that they had brought their own fold-up chairs. One family had even gone to the bother of pitching a tent. Wooden benches were provided for the rest of us. I sat down on one and watched a bike race. I don't think the clan warriors of old had bike races. 'Donald, see if ye can catch me on ma Chopper.' 'Ach, Ah'll leave ye fir dust on ma Grifter, Malcolm.' Some serious-looking Germans walked past waving tiny flags with Saltires on them. I was glad they were having fun.

Over at the Highland-dancing stage, the results from the Highland Fling were just in. The Highland Fling was created in 1792 in honour of the Duchess of Gordon. When the dancers put their hands over their heads they are depicting the antlers of a stag. The dancing steps are victory steps over the bodies of the slain. Highland dancing recalls bloody battle scenes. It's a gruesome kind of gracefulness. Next up was the Barracks Johnny.

All around the Games arena, pipers appeared to be competing for supremacy, some of them practising behind trees. Beside the Games arena was a fairground where children were having a hoot in the Haunted House. What with the racket from the amusements and the skirl of the bagpipes, my ears were taking a dreadful battering. After a while I tuned out and it became a bearable soundtrack to my afternoon. The piping competition was a curiosity to my novice eyes. There were these little huts dotted about the grounds. In each hut sat two men. They were the piping judges. The pipers walked slowly back and forth on small platforms in front of the huts and the judges scribbled down notes or scoffed sandwiches from their Tupperware boxes or just looked bored.

The pipes may be synonymous with Scotland but are thought to have originated in Egypt, where a basic chanter and drone were played together. Later a bag made of skin was added. The pipes were possibly played in England first before they were given a blast in Scotland. Now there's a thought. Perhaps it's another one to strike off the list of so-called Scottish inventions, a list that includes whisky and tartan. Soon all we Scots will be able to cling to is the fact that we dreamt up pasta. I don't care what the Italians say.

One of the piping competitions is the Piobaireachd (pronounced pea-broch). The piper is challenged to throw some variations into the performance. It's sort of piping improvisation. I'd no idea how the guy currently playing was getting on. I tried to gauge it by the faces of the two judges. One of them looked sort of half-interested. The other had a face like thunder.

There was some heavy shit going down in the main arena. CAUTION THROWING AREA warned a sign. The headliners, the Metallica of the Highland Games, are the heavy athletes, who lift heavy metal and heavy logs and throw them. The heavy events recall the clan chiefs testing the strength of their clansmen to see if they could rely on them in battle. Nowadays it's about personal bests and prize money. The heavy athletes compete for hours on end and represent the biggest draw for the Highland Games crowd because, let's face it, watching a man throw a tree trunk is marginally more interesting than watching a man play the bagpipes.

I watched the hammer throwing. The hammer flew through the air with the greatest of ease and landed with a dunt, taking a large divot out of the grass. I was mostly concerned for the photographer standing in front of the hammer throwers. I trusted he regularly photographed hammer throwers and knew what he was doing and therefore knew where the hammers were going.

Hammer throwing is thought to have developed from black-smiths showing off in the auld days. 'A huge throw there from Peter Hart,' boomed the Birnam Highland Games MC. The crowd was in awe. It truly was a mighty chuck. 'And you can see now why Pete is in the lead.' We sure could. 'It looks like the pin's on the move.' It was too.

Next up was throwing the weight for distance. The weight was on the end of a chain. The thrower swung round in circles and on the third turn let go of the chain, coming to a dead stop at the trig and watching the weight soar. It was very graceful. Rhythm seemed as important as power. Pete wiped his brow with a towel and took off his T-shirt. He was down to a vest, with his arm muscles bulging. He crouched, twirled three times and over his head went the weight with his army of fans cheering. Not only was he the favourite; he was the crowd's favourite.

'I'm told Pete was going for the ground record,' notified the MC, 'and he may well have done that with an awesome throw.' The tape measure was out. It looked good. It *was* good. Pete sat down on a tool box that was possibly his lunch box. He devoured a banana. The caber tossing – the 'Enter Sandman' moment of the heavy events – was yet to come. One heavy event that's no longer part of the Highland Games is twisting the legs off a cow, and you can see why.

The heavy men had moved on to putting the stone. 'A magnificent putt!' cried the MC. It was Pete again. The putt is thrown with one hand from the front of the shoulders with a short run up before the release. It looks like hard work but Pete was making it look easy. Following the next challenge of throwing the weight over the bar – where it looks like the thrower is going to be clobbered on the head by the weight on the way down – it was caber time, which promised to be even more thrilling than hammer time.

The caber is tapered at one end and from there it is lifted by the tosser – he doesn't mind me calling him a tosser – who 'rests' the caber against his shoulder. He then runs and gets rid of the thing. If he does it right, the caber spins over and lands at 12 o'clock. Caber tossing is not about how far you can toss, it's about the straightest toss, and 12 o'clock can't be beaten. Caber tossing has its roots in forestry, when the easiest way to get a felled tree trunk over a burn was to chuck it end-over-end.

Pete the Invincible gave the first toss, managing 11 o'clock and getting the thumbs up. The next guy didn't give a toss, the caber slipping through his fingers like a greasy pole. Not that I'm criticising him. At least he was capable of picking the caber up before dropping it. 'Try it at home with something nice and easy – a broomstick handle,' the MC suggested to us. It's not really the same, is it?

Riffing some more off the caber tossing, the MC declared, 'If this has whetted your appetite for competition, we still have the World Haggis Eating Championships! If you've never seen it before, believe me, it's carnage.' That sounded good.

Ahead of the offal scoffing, I went and had a look inside a big tent where they had the programme from the 1832 Highland Games. The events and prizes were listed. The winner of the Piobaireachd got a handsome mounted pipe and the runner-up got a sporran molloch. The best-dressed Highlander received a silver mounted snuff mull. And the best tosser of the bar got not a lifetime ban but a silver brooch.

It was haggis time. Up for grabs were the world title and a bottle of whisky. Track events had been suspended temporarily and plates were being placed on the table. This was pretty exciting. There was a last call for entrants. A young boy begged his dad to have a go. 'I suppose it's free food,' said the dad, showing off some impeccable Scots credentials. 'You can win it!' said the boy. 'I suppose I could hide some behind my ears,' said his dad, who bit the bullet and went and put his name down. I hoped he wasn't really going to stash some haggis behind his lugs. He was bound to be caught, and his son would be ashamed of him. I had no intention of entering. I love haggis but I'd no one to show off to. If my wife or a friend had been there, I'd have given it a go, I like to think. But instead, I stayed behind the ropes like the big coward I am. I asked one of the Games officials if there was a secret to speed-eating haggis. There wasn't. 'Ye jist open yer mooth and stick it in.'

About 20 World Title contenders gathered round the table. A man approached with a big tray of steaming haggis covered in tea towels. The individual haggises were placed on the plates. Forks were on hand too but the forks were there to fool you. 'With a fork you'll never win,' a man-in-the-know next to me whispered. You had to eat your haggis with your bare hands (or you weren't a true Scotsman). The gun was fired and the faces plunged into hot mushy haggis. It was carnage, right enough. What a mess they made.

How hard can it be, eating an entire haggis in a hurry? Pretty hard. Some of the hopefuls were truly struggling early on. They'd seriously underestimated Scotland's national dish. I was torn between hoping they'd bring their haggis back up again and hoping they wouldn't. It would have been sick but it would have been funny. Wait a minute though. Someone had their hand up. And in their hand was an empty haggis skin. We had a winner! He'd gobbled the lot, leaving the rest trailing in his wake. He was local man Willie Robertson. He'd won the title four years ago. His time today was two minutes and five seconds. Willie posed with his bottle of whisky for his picture in the paper. I asked the World Haggis Eating Champion what his secret was. 'A big belly,' said his friend. 'A big mouth and a big belly,' corrected Willie.

The Highland Games was everything I had thought it would be, with a haggis twist. What I can say about the Highland Games is that it's better than watching Scottish football.

My Lovely Horse

– *Festival of the Horse and Boys' Ploughing Match, South Ronaldsay* –

My dad-in-law Dave dropped me off at Inverness bus station at stupid o'clock in the morning. We'd left Elgin in what felt like the middle of the night. I was going to Orkney for the day. I had reserved a seat on the daily coach tour from Inverness. Not that I was touring Orkney. I was going as far as St Margaret's Hope on South Ronaldsay for the annual Festival of the Horse and Boys' Ploughing Match. The coach driver was going to drop me off before continuing with the tourists to visit the standing stones and Skara Brae. The coach would pick me up again on the way back and return me to Inverness, from where I'd catch the last train to Elgin. This was the perfect plan: my penultimate festival, return transport, a flavour of a coach tour and, most importantly, I'd be back in Elgin to see Clare and look in on a sleeping Isabella before the end of the night.

I boarded the coach with an assortment of Scandinavians, Americans, Italians and Eastern Europeans. There wasn't a seat to spare. We were soon on our way north to John O' Groats. I fell asleep and woke up in the sprawling and sparsely populated county of Sutherland, half of which I own. The girl sitting in front of me was busy with her camera taking pictures of every second field. I'd say she was on a field trip but that would be a terrible joke.

A gargantuan German woman heaved herself out of her two seats and squeezed down the aisle towards the coach driver. How I hadn't noticed her before, I don't know. How the coach was still moving was a wonder to me as well. The woman was wider than the coach. As she huffed and puffed, her more than ample sides whacked the heads of passengers left and right, waking a few of them up. When she finally reached the driver – the coach was tipped up on its front wheels by now – she asked him to stop. He asked her what for and she barked that she needed the toilet. The driver explained that he couldn't stop because we were on a tight schedule to make the ferry from John O' Groats. The German woman was having none of it. She insisted he stop, even though we were in the middle of Sutherland and there was nowhere to stop. The driver drew her attention to the fact that there was a toilet on board, halfway down the aisle and down a few steps. But he sounded as unconvinced as the rest of us felt that she'd actually fit in it. The German woman harrumphed some more, somehow managed to turn round and forced her way back down the aisle while several heads ducked out of the way. She got to the steps to the toilet. I couldn't even look. Ten minutes later, I heard a door shut. She'd shrunk herself in there. After a while, the door creaked open and she manoeuvred her way back to her two seats where she remained for the rest of the journey, thank goodness.

I wasn't at all disappointed with John O' Groats, because I knew it was going to be shit. I'd never heard anybody say a good thing about it. They should call it John O' For God's Sake. It's such an eyesore. I'd only been there five minutes and already I was desperate to leave. Fortunately I'd be on the next ferry, crossing six miles of sea to the southern tip of Orkney. John O' Groats has one of those wacky signposts that tell you how many miles you are from various faraway places. The North Pole was 2,200 miles away and probably more hospitable than John O' Groats. It was 20,875 miles to New Zealand, which I'd always wanted to know. The genius of this signpost was that it could be altered for the John O' Groats tourist. A new sign was going up for Sheffield. For a few pounds you could have your picture taken to show all your friends that you were in John O' Groats and thus miles from your home town. The hairy biker posed and pointed at Sheffield as if to say, 'Hey, I'm in John O' Groats and look how far away from Sheffield I am.' I didn't bother finding out if the man in charge of the lucrative signpost business had a sign for Hopeman.

I climbed aboard the *Pentland Venture*, but only after waiting for the colossal German woman from the coach to board first. I'd wanted to see what would happen. The ferry was still afloat and I was on the next leg of my journey, destined for South Ronaldsay. It couldn't be half as grim as John O' Groats, surely.

South Ronaldsay isn't much to look at when you arrive on the ferry – just a couple of half-fallen-down stone buildings – but it still looked nicer than John O' Groats. There was another coach and a new driver waiting for the tour group I'd almost forgotten I was part of. No sign of the German woman. She must have become lodged in the ferry toilet. When she finally got out, she'd be back in John O' Groats, poor woman. I was only on this second coach for the briefest of spells because it wasn't far to St Margaret's Hope, but our amazing driver packed in some excellent onboard commentary before we reached my stop and the others carried on to the standing stones or whatever it was they were doing. In the space of ten minutes I found out an awful lot about Orkney.

I learned, for instance, that the sheep on South Ronaldsay outnumber the people ten to one, and that, in terms of population and size, it's 2km per person (meaning people have awful big gardens but the ten sheep in each garden must chew the grass bare). I learned that there are 70 islands on Orkney. That we were currently on the same latitude as St Petersburg in Russia. But that Orkney doesn't get as much snow. I learned that the winter temperatures in Orkney are fairly moderate and that it's mainly due to the North Atlantic Drift – or Gulf Stream if you prefer. I learned that the average summer temperature in Orkney is 14° Centigrade. That the average winter temperature is 4° Centigrade. That the population of Orkney is just under 20,000 and, of those, 15,000 live on 'mainland' Orkney, the largest island of the group. That we were 300 miles from Norway and 700 miles from London. 'There are those who would like Orkney to go back to Norway,' added the driver. 'They either don't drink or don't know the price of drink, because, if they did, they wouldn't want to be part of Norway.' I learned that the main industry in Orkney is agriculture but that tourism is catching up fast and should overtake it soon. That there are approximately 100,000 beef cattle on Orkney and, in any year, 30,000 are sold to the Scottish mainland and beyond. That there are up to 150,000 sheep. That the sheep in North Ronaldsay live off seaweed and taste pretty good. That, with all these animals to feed, the main crop on Orkney is grass. That there is also some barley grown for animal feed. That the animals spend seven months indoors because of the long dark nights of winter. That for animals – and humans – the winter weather in Orkney is dominated by two things: wind and rain. That St Margaret's Hope comes from the Norse word for haven or harbour and that St Margaret was Queen Margaret, the wife of King Malcolm of Scotland. That there was once a chapel to Margaret in the village. That, in the nineteenth century, St Margaret's Hope was, like other villages, very busy with the herring fishing. That there would have been 25 to 30 shops when the village was at its busiest. And that there are now four shops, two hotels and a pub.

The coach driver pulled up at the top of the road leading down into St Margaret's Hope. Time for me to hop off. 'If you can be here for half-four,' the driver said, 'I'll try and remember to look out for you.' Well, try and remember, would you? Otherwise I'd be stuck. I thanked him and began walking down the road into St Margaret's Hope. Inverness felt like yesterday. What an odd morning I was having.

The likeable town of St Margaret's Hope lies at the head of a sheltered bay. I warmed to it straight away and had a look about the place. The menu in the window of the local shoreside restaurant had me salivating. Home-cured, seaweed-fed North Ronaldsay mutton, anyone? Roasted wolf fish? Steamed ling and seared Orkney scallops? If only I had someone to dine with . . . and more money. All I had was a tuna sandwich in a Tupperware box. Never mind. The important thing was that my wife had made that sandwich. She's so good to me.

A sign in the post office window brought some bad news to this nice town. The local gardens had, once again, been vanda-lised. 'The lower garden gate has been irretrievably damaged. Someone has broken the lower spars and scattered them in the flower borders. This very gate featured in the photo of circa 1930s but now features on police records!'

I found the beautiful village square and Cromarty Hall where the Festival of the Horse was to take place, but I was early. I nipped into the pub around the corner where they were doing brisk business with their fish soup. One man at the bar ordered a plate and opened his wallet. 'Give me the blue note,' said the barman, taking the fiver and placing it in the till. 'Here's five-pence change and I'm no' even wearing a mask to rob you. Fish costs a bit these days.' There were no grumbles from the customers. They were happy to pay for a good bowl of home-made fish soup. I considered trying some myself but I'd not long scoffed my tuna sandwich. I ordered a pint instead. It was good not to be cooped up on a coach or rocking around on a ferry.

The Festival of the Horse and Boys' Ploughing Match is – as it sounds – a two-parter. It dates back to the latter half of the nineteenth century and its origin lies in farming. (Remember, fact-fiends, agriculture is Orkney's main industry, though tourism is catching up fast.) Before tractors replaced Clydesdale horses, hard-working ploughmen occasionally showed off their skills and horses in competition. All over Orkney there were ploughing contests. The ploughmen would also spend time grooming their horses, decorating the tails and manes with ribbons and polishing up the brass on the harnesses.

The Boys' Ploughing Match came from sons copying their fathers. The boys used makeshift ploughs, perhaps a stick with an ox's hoof tied to it. They would practise their ploughing and hope to become great ploughmen themselves one day. In South Ronaldsay, in the 1920s, a local blacksmith made the first miniature metal ploughs for the boys to get their hands on. Eventually, with modernisation, there was no need for the manual ploughing of fields and the imitation ploughing by the boys amounted to nothing more than a reminder of a bygone era. The tradition of ploughing is still reflected every year in the Boys' Ploughing Match which takes place on the Sands o' Wright, a few miles from St Margaret's Hope.

The other part of the festival, the Festival of the Horse, couldn't be more different, though it is linked to the ploughing. Boys who were too young to plough were dressed up as horses. Their Sunday suits would be adapted and decorated. Over the years, this portrayal of the Clydesdale horses became more and more elaborate. Today it's the young girls of South Ronaldsay who are transformed into horses in a curious show of pageantry. In the dedicated effort to resemble the horses that once pulled the ploughs, the girls wear harnesses, tails and even blinkers, with their ornate outfits festooned in buttons, flowers and brooches. Some of these horse costumes are handed down generations. They might be adapted each year for the latest Festival of the Horse, where the 'horses' are judged in two categories: best harness and best decoration. The Festival of the Horse precedes the Boys' Ploughing Match and you must either be resident in

South Ronaldsay to take part or have had a parent or grandparent take part in the past. To the outsider, the Festival of the Horse – if not the Boys' Ploughing Match – may seem bizarre. It had me thinking of Father Ted. But I wasn't here to mock. I was here to watch and enjoy the day as the locals do when the Festival of the Horse and Boys' Ploughing Match come around.

I went over to the hall and found Moira Budge, the committee secretary, whose daughter Amy-Jayne was taking part in the Festival of the Horse. Moira showed me some of the horse costumes that would be worn in the hope of impressing this year's judges. She explained how they'd developed from frugal beginnings.

'The horses were very basic to begin with as material was scarce and expensive to buy anything fancy,' said Moira. 'The Sunday suits were used to sew on some decorations, and a collar was added. Then it would have been removed again afterwards. It's jist to try and copy what the real horses had. You see, you've got the harness and the tail, and the blinkers that the horses would have had. Maybe a bridle as well. The troosers are the hind legs and there's wee cuffs that go roond the feet, ken, like the feathers o' the Clydesdale horses. And you might have rosettes or peedie wee ribbons. I haven't done anything with this one.' She was holding up her daughter's costume. 'I keep thinking I should try and do something a bit more ornate. You'll find some outfits that are so covered in decorations and ornaments it can be . . .'

Too much?

'Well, some folk say it. You might get some that are really very plain wi' a few sparkly bits. They're a' different. Some don't have ears. Some don't have bridles.'

I let Moira get on with her preparations and went and joined the crowd that had begun to gather in the square. The MC made us welcome and introduced the live band. 'Ladies and gentlemen, it's fine that the sun's come through. There's tea and coffee in the hall, don't be shy. I'll hand you over to the Braelanders.'

'You're lucky we've got no tapes or CDs,' joked the lead singer. 'You'll just go away with bad ears. Pit it down as an experience. Dance if you want.' The accordionist launched into it.

The plough boys – some in boiler suits and wellies, others in jeans and T-shirts – sat in front of us on benches, with their miniature ploughs in front of them, real intricate pieces which would be put to work soon on the beach, after they had been scrutinised by the judges.

The Braelanders wrapped up a barnstorming number. 'Put your request down on a twenty-pound note and we'll try and get it played.' But The Braelanders had to stop for now. It was time for the Festival of the Horse.

The 'horses' were piped out the door of the hall in all their finery, their fetlocks blowing in the wind. They were all colour and sparkle and you could see the battle going on between the more traditional and the wildly elaborate. Those harnesses round their necks looked like hard work. I'd never seen anything like it. They paraded, they were judged and Moira's daughter won a prize. 'You did alright,' smiled Moira. 'Second – that's not bad. You're back in the money.'

After the horses, the ploughs were inspected. 'The best-kept plough isn't necessarily the bonniest painted one,' a plough expert told me. 'It's jist one that's good work, not stuck, with plenty of grease so it'll no stick on the sand. Yer looking for no rust and a smooth-running wheel.' Once the ploughs had been rated and the results announced, the horses and the ploughmen, the girls and boys, paraded in front of their proud parents and grandparents and the several tourists who had stumbled across the scene and perhaps were trying to work it out.

The scene then switched from the square to the Sands o'

Wright. Thanks to Moira, I managed to cadge a lift down to the beach in a mini-bus. 'I'm Gary from Glasgow,' I said to the driver. 'I'm Eric fae Orkney,' he replied. I sat in the back with his dog at my feet. It wasn't long and we were at the beach.

I walked across the gorgeous Sands o' Wright with the wind in my face. An area of sand had been marked off. Each boy had a patch to plough and had 45 minutes to finish up. They were expected to plough straight and even. 'Right boys . . .' They were raring to go. What touched me was that this was a father-and-son scene. The boys bent over their ploughs, their dads giving advice.

I wasn't on the Sands o' Wright any more. I was back on Hopeman beach. The tide was out and I was walking towards the Daisy Rock with my dad.

The Boldest Swingers in Town

— *The Fireballs, Stonehaven* —

It was time for the last — and the first — festival of the year: Hogmanay in Stonehaven. Never mind Edinburgh's street party; Stonehaven's wild celebration was the sort of thing that made Scotland stand out — swingers soaking their fiery balls in the sea after midnight.

I'd come to watch, as had 10,000 others. The mood was warm and generous. It made you mind the cold less, though in fact it was pretty mild for the last day in December. Things were going to heat up too when the swingers swung into action.

Accompanying me on the final leg of my year-long festival journey were The Manny Willox and The Manny Nicklas. The Manny Nicklas is a teacher at the same Aberdeen school as The Manny Willox. The Manny Nicklas's first name is Stephen, but I can't be calling him Stephen, him being a teacher and all that.

The Manny Willox was full of the joys of Hogmanay. 'Just think, that's another year of your life you've wasted.' He can be dead droll, can The Manny Willox.

After a long search for a parking space, The Manny Willox parked his Batmobile on the outskirts of Stonehaven. We'd been advised to turn up early and, as far as we were concerned, we *had* turned up early, but it was still a struggle. The fireballs are popular these days. The two Mannys and I — or should I say the twa Mannys and I — followed the rest of the voyeurs to the harbour, where the swinging was scheduled to start on the stroke of midnight.

'You're in for a treat,' I said to The Manny Nicklas, who's

from Paisley. Stonehaven is a wonderful coastal town with a stunning setting, wedged between cliffs, fifteen miles south of Aberdeen. The Fireballs are the jam on the buttery. Or, if you can't stomach jammy butteries, the icing on the cake.

They've been swinging fireballs in Stonehaven since the mid-nineteenth century. The fireballs are basically cages made of fencing wire, filled with rags, twigs, cardboard, coal, pine cones, old jumpers, whatever combustibles come to hand. Each swinger has their own recipe. Plastic and rubber are avoided. The fireball swinger doesn't want melted plastic dripping down their neck. The contents of the cage are doused in paraffin. No petrol gets anywhere near the fireball as the swingers want as low a heat as possible.

The day before the ceremony, I'd spoken to Martin Sim, a veteran swinger looking forward to his 32nd Fireballs ceremony. Martin is vice-chairman of the organising committee and runs a hair salon in Stonehaven. 'You want to control the heat and stop the reek,' explained Martin, talking about fireballs and not hairdrying. 'We have to walk with the fireballs so you want to be able to breathe the next morning. You don't want to be coughing your guts up.'

The fireball cage has a wire handle between two and three feet long, enabling the swinger to swing their fireball above their head as they march down the street to the delight of the crowd. The length of handle depends on how confident the swinger is. The shorter the handle, the hotter your ears get.

A lot of the fireballs are made well in advance, but there are always one or two last-minute efforts. 'They're all checked to be roadworthy,' said Martin. Fireballs have to be certified, just like the swingers. A few years back, the alarm bells were ringing. 'We could see problems. There were safety issues,' admitted Martin. The fireballs were an accident waiting to happen. So a committee was formed and the organisation of the event was tightened. 'We put in place robust safety measures. Some of the cages weren't up to the mark. Now we have more controls and general rules of thumb that ensure safety is adhered to. We make sure that the fireballs are robust and can stand what we put them through.'

Swinging a fireball is, as you might imagine, demanding. It requires dexterity, strength and concentration. Fireballs can weigh anything from 10 to 20lbs. 'It's quite tiring,' said Martin, 'but you want to perform to a reasonable standard. The adrenalin pushes you. You prepare yourself for it, but it doesn't matter how many trial runs you have. That thing has a life of its own!'

The swingers are men and women, ranging from teenagers to pensioners. Whole families take part in the ceremony. I asked Martin how you become a fireball swinger. 'If you've been involved in the sidelines, you're eligible to put your name forward. Maybe you've served as a marshal for a couple of years. It used to be that you had to be born in Stonehaven, but we're not bothered about that now. It's too restrictive. Still, you have to stay in the local area. New people come in. Some will stop and others will start. And the tradition continues. It's not about one person. It's about the mass.

'A lot of people would love to swing, but we don't want just anybody doing it. We don't want any loose cannons not doing it properly. That can cause problems. You need to know the routine. It's not for the personal glory – waving it to your friends and treating it as a laugh. You can't fool around with these things. Some do it once and never again. It's about putting the time in.'

What's best to wear when you're playing with fire? 'Anything you fancy wearing,' said Martin. 'Everything from boiler suits to kilts. There's one guy who persists in wearing T-shirt and shorts. He's a skinny lad, too. You'd think those legs wouldn't survive anywhere.'

Martin couldn't wait to get started. He put himself in the picture and painted it for me. 'The guy ahead moves off . . . and then it's your turn. The flickering flames on the walls . . . it's a wonderful thing to be involved in. It's amazing.'

I said I couldn't wait to see the finale when they fling their fireballs into the sea. That was the part I most wanted to witness. 'That's brilliant, chucking them in the harbour,' laughed Martin, 'mainly just to put them out. You give your all and hurl it in the water. It's quite spectacular.'

Like a lot of old customs still kicking around in Scotland, the keepers of the tradition don't truly know what it's about. Why did the locals of Stonehaven take to swinging burning balls? There are a few fireball theories flying around. It could be the old routine of burning off the bad spirits, or another midwinter festival beckoning the sun. Interestingly, there's the tale of a shooting star once streaking across the night sky, preceding a good harvest. Since the people could not command shooting stars, they set about mimicking them with home-made fireballs. Personally, I think it had nothing to do with shooting stars or welcoming the sun. I think they just wanted to try their hand at making fireballs. Martin pointed out that burning away the old year was a fishing tradition. Stonehaven – like Burghead – was a thriving fishing community, back when Scotland had thriving fishing communities.

The fireballs burn half an hour before they're extinguished in the North Sea, but they used to burn a lot longer. The swingers would whirl their fireballs for a few yards before stopping at a friend's house, leaving their fireball on the doorstep and popping inside for a New Year dram. They'd then pick up where they left off.

Enthusiasm for the fireballs had dampened somewhat by the 1960s when very few swingers got their hands hot. But there remained a few die-hards who were eventually able to persuade more and more people to take part in the ancient ceremony and the numbers were brought back up again. The Fireballs has never been cancelled and it's never been so popular.

It has to be controlled though, as Martin mentioned. It can't be spontaneous like it might have been a long time ago: 'I'm just going to swing my fireball down the street.' Volunteer marshals and crowd barriers are needed to guarantee safety and ensure the procession runs like clockwork.

You don't even need to be in Stonehaven to see the Fireballs (though it remains the best way of seeing them). A webcam means people can watch the Fireballs from anywhere in the world. In recent years, the presence of the TV cameras has allowed the rest of Scotland to witness some of the swinging from their living rooms. Martin is not a huge fan of the TV cameras. If the TV people had their way, they'd be doing the Fireballs twice over, in order to get the best shots. 'They ask "Could you do that?" and I say "This is what we do."' Any self-respecting swinger wouldn't be told how to swing.

The Mannies Willox and Nicklas and I walked down Stone-haven High Street past the TV crew, their arms full of wires as they readied themselves for the filming of a northern spectacular. They'd be alright, the TV people, so long as they didn't stop a swinger and ask them to swing their fireball anti-clockwise rather than clockwise.

Yes, the preparations were in full swing, so to speak, and the metal barriers were already in place to prevent people from getting their hair singed. A group of girls leaned out the window of a top-floor flat. They were having a party and they were singing Meatloaf. 'I would do anything for love,' they yelled. The three of us waved up and they laughed back at us.

This was one of those New Years where you got an extra second – a 'leap second' at midnight – to put the Earth's rotation back in line with the atomic clocks. What would we do with that extra second in the streets of Stonehaven? Kick a stranger in the shins? Give them a New Year kiss? Would we even notice the extra second?

We shifted from the time conundrum to the subject of time

travel and a discussion of *Dr Who*. I didn't watch *Dr Who*, but said I would more than likely be a fan of his Stonehaven counterpart, if he existed. (Not that Dr Who does either, but you know what I mean.) A Stonehaven Timelord, I ruminated, would speak – or even spik – in the Doric tongue. He'd be called Dr Fa. The Manny Willox disagreed. He said a Stonehaven Timelord would be called Dr Foo. The Manny Nicklas – not originating from the north-east – didn't have a particular opinion on the matter. He'd no idea what a Stonehaven Timelord should be called and probably didn't care. The Manny Willox and I did care. 'Fa,' I repeated. 'Foo,' countered The Manny Willox. 'Fa.' 'Foo.' 'Fa.' Foo.' 'Fuck off,' we both said at the same time. And to think he was a teacher. I chastised him and he cursed me again. I didn't deserve that. I decided that Dr Fa should be consigned to the BBC archives.

It was 11 o'clock. An hour (and a second) to go. The harbour area was already heaving. The pubs might have had something to do with it. I fought my way into one of them and called for three pints. We drank them outside, sitting on a wall, looking out at the water. This was the life. It was very pleasant. I was full of the joys of Hogmanay and looking forward to the pyrotechnics. Around us, I could hear French people, Germans, Spaniards. The Fireballs was now an international affair. It had gone way beyond Stonehaven. We even had a man from Paisley. This festival had no difficulty attracting tourists. The Stonehaven Pipe Band struck up and people cheered. Suddenly it felt even more like Hogmanay. I felt the hip flask in my pocket. It could wait till the bells. Hogmanay and Glenlivet were made for each other.

I don't know why, but I suddenly thought of *Seinfeld*, one of my favourite comedy shows. In one episode, George's dad, Frank, introduces his alternative version of Christmas: Festivus. 'A Festivus for the rest of us!' At Festivus, you can eat whatever you want. During the traditional Airing of Grievances, you gather round the table and let your family know how much they've disappointed you in the past year. I wondered what Frank's take on Hogmanay would be. Maybe he'd call it Hogmafest. 'A Hogmafest for the rest of us!' At Hogmafest you can drink whatever you want. During the traditional Airing of Injustices, you gather round the table and let your family know how it's just not fair.

When we'd finished our pints, we looked around for what we thought might be the best place to see the fireballs being hurled into the water. Well, the harbour would be good. We found space on the wall next to the slipway and plonked ourselves there for the duration. We'd secured a prime spot for the fiery finale. You had to think of positioning when it came to the swinging. I'd rather have been more carefree, but with so many spectators I didn't want to be in danger of missing everything. And plenty other people had the same idea. You grab a spot and you hold onto it. I made myself as comfortable as I could on the wall and The Manny Nicklas sat next to me. The Manny Willox had to stand. Served him right. Dr Foo indeed.

We chatted and waited and waited and chatted. Then a roar went up. The fireballs had been lit. We couldn't see the bloody things but they were on fire alright. Unless the crowd was cheering about the extra second. Suddenly the bells were ringing and we were all shaking hands and hugging each other and wishing each other a Happy New Year. While trying not to fall off the wall onto the sand, I sorted out a pair of drams for The Manny Nicklas and myself. I'd have given one to The Manny Willox but he was our designated driver and would have to wait until we got back to Aberdeen. He was okay with that.

Soon the first swinger strutted down the slipway, swinging his fireball in an almost nonchalant manner. He gave it one last swing before firing it into the dark. The fireball sailed through the black like a comet and then splashed down into the water. It was an incredible sight and I settled back to watch it occur over and over again, fireballs plunging into the sea. It was mesmerising. It was beautiful. And calming.

I was watching the Fireballs in Stonehaven and I was with friends but I was away now in another place. Maybe the whisky was taking me there, but I suspect it was merely the time of year. And I was only doing what a lot of other people were doing, whether they were here in Stonehaven, or in any other town, village or city throughout Scotland and across the world. I was thinking about how my year had gone and wondering what the next had in store for me. I was thinking about family and friends. About Clare and Isabella back in Elgin. About my mam in Hopeman, and my brother and sister. And I was thinking about my dad, but not in the way I'd done a year ago when I lay on a couch in Kirkwall feeling sorry for myself. I missed him as much as I did then – I always would – but it wasn't all grief. Other brighter feelings had come to the fore. He'd have loved this, the Fireballs, and I wished he was here sitting on this wall with me, sharing a dram by the harbour. He was a man of the sea; he liked a party and he enjoyed seeing people do daft things like this. I heard him laugh. Not in the real sense; I was just remembering how my dad laughed. I was glad I was facing the water so no one could see my tears. But what's wrong with crying? I wasn't the only one crying right now. I wiped my jacket sleeve across my watery eyes and watched the fireworks illuminate Stonehaven. You got a proper sense of the place, the dramatic cliffs, this fantastic location for welcoming in the New Year. I felt the thud of the fireworks in my heart. It was almost overpowering.

I had crossed the festival finish line. In many ways it had been a difficult year but in one way, the safe arrival of Isabella, it had been the best ever year. And, as far as the festivals go, I could look back with fondness on all those new experiences and new faces. Scotland has its faults – we all have our faults – but Scotland is worth celebrating, and that's what festivals are for: celebration.

With the fireballs put out and the fireworks over, everybody started making for the pubs, their houses or their cars. Martin had enjoyed taking part in his 32nd Fireballs ceremony. He'd made quite an impression on the crowd with the digital clock round his neck. He'd found it in the Argos catalogue and thought – twenty quid, I'm having that. 'I set it more or less to the time. People were laughing and cheering. I did a wee turn.'

For Martin, the Fireballs had been another success. 'It certainly went very well. There were no problems from start to finish. The weather was perfect. There was a bit of confusion before the start, but it all came together. It was very, very busy. Numbers-wise, that's a huge crowd, bigger than I think it's ever been. But we'd do it anyway.'

Dan had said the same thing about The Clavie. *We'd do it anyway*.

I commented to Martin that the swingers had made it look effortless. 'As long as it *looks* effortless,' he laughed.

Stonehaven had brought in the Bells as Stonehaven does. 'Edinburgh and Glasgow have their Hogmanay parties and they're rich enough in their own way,' said Martin, 'but this is more community orientated and you feel part of something. There's a certain amount of tradition here that people like – and it won't stop now.'

The fireballs will burn for a long time in Stonehaven.

Thankfully, in the morning, my head did not resemble a fireball. I hadn't overdone it at Hogmanay. I hadn't underdone it either. It was just right. I'd been in a more reflective mood than a wanting-to-get-drunk mood. I felt all the better for it as I tackled one of The Manny Willox's excellent cooked breakfasts.

Then The Manny Willox, The Manny Nicklas and I got in the car and left Aberdeen for the foot of Bennachie. By noon on New Year's Day, we were in the clouds and I could see clearly.

Thanks a bunch

Colin Keldie (Visit Orkney); Robert Leslie (Doonie); Gary, Edgar and Sigurd Gibson (Uppies); Dan Ralph (Brocher); Elma Johnson; Douglas Sinclair; Annalene Williamson; Will Roome; Keith Belleville; Nick Rodger; Nick Rodger's mam Marion; Nick Rodger's brother Chris; Nick Rodger's nephew Wilf; Nick Rodger's pal Robin (Gizzard); Shirley Currie; The Burry Man (John Nicol); Dave Laing; Moira Budge; Martin Sim; Jack Wood; Stan at Jenny Brown Associates; Neville, Andrew and everyone at Birlinn; The Manny Willox; Nayland Smith (another Brocher); Jonathan Davidson; Brian Noble; The Manny Nicklas; Prince Rogers Nelson; Mam, The Buzz (wise up); Herb Clumpy III; Adele; The Buzz (wise up again); and Clare and Isabella Rose for putting up with my gallivanting. Coming home was the sweetest thing.

I must thank James Alexander Sutherland too for all that he's given me.

Read more

If you want to learn more about The Ba', check out John D. M. Robertson's *The Kirkwall Ba': From the Water to the Wall* (Dunedin Academic Press).

And if you want to find out more about Scottish festivals and customs in general, then have a look for *It's An Old Scottish Custom* by Francis Drake-Carnell (Peter Davies), if you can get your hands on it, or I can always flog you my copy for £978.53. Okay then, make it £978.

Keep capering

Kirkwallians, Lerwegians, Langholmites and all you other caperers – even Brochers – keep capering!